SONG OF KARMAPA
The Aspiration of the
Mahamudra of True Meaning
by Lord Rangjung Dorjé

Books by Traleg Kyabgon

Integral Buddhism: Developing All Aspects of One's Personhood, Shogam Publications, 2018

King Doha: Saraha's Advice to a King, Shogam Publications, 2018

Letter to a Friend: Nagarjuna's Classic Text, Shogam Publications, 2018

Moonbeams of Mahamudra: The Classic Meditation Manual, Shogam Publications, 2015

Karma: What it is, What it isn't, and Why it matters, Shambhala Publications, 2015

Four Dharmas of Gampopa, KTD Publications, 2013

Asanga's Abhidharmasamuccaya, KTD Publications, 2013

Ninth Karmapa Wangchuk Dorjé's Ocean Of Certainty, KTD Publications, 2011

Influence of Yogacara on Mahamudra, KTD Publications, 2010

The Practice of Lojong: Cultivating Compassion through Training the Mind, Shambhala Publications, 2007

Mind at Ease: Self-Liberation through Mahamudra Meditation, Shambhala Publications, 2004

Benevolent Mind: A Manual in Mind Training, Zhisil Chokyi Ghatsal, 2003

The Essence of Buddhism: An Introduction to Its Philosophy and Practice, Shambhala Publications, 2002 & 2014

Photo facing page: Traleg Kyabgon Rinpoche the Ninth

SONG OF KARMAPA

The Aspiration of the Mahamudra of True Meaning
by Lord Rangjung Dorjé

Translation and Oral Commentary
Traleg Kyabgon

Forewords by
Ogyen Trinley Dorjé, 17th Karmapa
and Khenpo Karthar Rinpoche

SHOGAM
PUBLICATIONS
2018

Shogam Publications Pty Ltd
PO Box 239 Ballarat, Victoria, Australia, 3353
www.shogam.org
info@shogam.com

Copyright © Felicity Lodro
First Edition

All rights reserved. No part of this publication may be reproduced in any form or by any means electronic or mechanical, including photocopying, recording, or by any information storage and retrieval system without prior permission in writing from the publisher. Enquiries should be made to the publisher.

Shogam Publications Pty Ltd has made every effort to contact the copyright holder of all material not owned by the publisher reproduced herein, interested parties may contact the publisher for further information.

Printed in Australia and the United States of America

Edited by David Bennett

Designed by David Bennett

National Library of Australia
Kyabgon, Traleg, 1955
Song of Karmapa: The Aspiration of the Mahamudra of True Meaning by Lord Rangjung Dorjé

Printed book ISBN: 978-0-6481148-4-0 (paperback)
E-book ISBN: 978-0-6481293-8-7

DEDICATION

To those aspiring to understand the true meaning and realize the nature of the mind, one's authentic condition, and to my extraordinary teacher, Traleg Kyabgon Rinpoche IX, the embodiment of *The Aspiration of the Mahamudra of True Meaning*.

Contents

Foreword by Ogyen Trinley Dorjé, 17th Karmapa	ix
Foreword by Khenpo Karthar Rinpoche	xi
Biography of Author	xiii
Acknowledgements	xvii
Editor's Introduction and Biography	xviii
The Root Verses	1
Section One: The Overview *Verses One – Two*	6
Section Two: The Correct Basis for Embarking on the Path *Verses Three – Four*	13
Section Three: The Means of Realizing the Path *Verse Five*	20
Section Four: The Path *Verse Six*	26
Section Five: How to Cultivate the Spiritual Path *Verses Seven – Twenty-three*	33
Section Six: Fruition *Verses Twenty-four – Twenty-five*	94
Notes	100
Bibliography	111
Terms and Names	113
Glossary	116
Index	123

Foreword

Within the Karma Kamtsang, the Traleg Tulku lineage holds particular, historical significance and can be traced back to Saltong Shogam, one of the "Three Men from Kham," close disciples of Lord Gampopa, who received the transmission of both Vajrayana and Mahamudra instructions directly from him.

The Ninth Traleg Rinpoche was recognized as a small child by the Sixteenth Gyalwang Karmapa. However, like many Tibetans at that time, his childhood was disrupted by the upheavals in Tibet, and he faced great difficulties. He had to flee Tibet for India, where he completed his traditional monastic education in Buddhist philosophy, studying both the Karma Kagyü and the Drukpa Kagyü traditions, before moving to Australia in 1980.

During his lifetime, Rinpoche had to adapt to alien cultures and a lifestyle very different from that of previous Traleg Rinpoches. His mastery of the English language, his scholarship, his studies at university level in western philosophy and comparative religion, and his personal experiences, all led him to develop a deep understanding of the western mind which enabled him to reach many students and become a highly effective Dharma teacher in the West.

The Third Karmapa, Rangjung Dorjé, also died before he reached sixty, yet, in the 900-year history of the Karmapa lineage, he is probably the most influential of all the Karmapas, renowned not just within the Karma Kamtsang but highly respected by other Kagyü traditions and by different lineages such as the Nyingma and Jonang. His composition Aspiration of the Mahamudra of True Meaning is a complete guide to the practice of Mahamudra. It clearly explains the view of Mahamudra, the ground, the path and the result, based on the experience of a fully realized master. Not only was the Third Karmapa a realized master but he had eighty students who also fully realized the Mahamudra under his instruction.

When the Ninth Traleg Rinpoche passed away at such a young age, people were shocked and saddened. Now a special effort is being made to preserve his teachings. I would like to thank all those who are engaged in the process of collating and publishing these teachings so that Traleg Rinpoche's extraordinary ability to communicate the Dharma is not lost but made available to all his students and a wider audience.

17th Karmapa
Ogyen Trinley Dorjé
25th May 2018

Foreword

༁ སྐྱབས་རྗེ་ཁྲ་ལེག་རིན་པོ་ཆེ་མཆོག་ནི་དེས་པ་དོན་གྱི་ཕྱག་
ཆེན་མངོན་དུ་གྱུར་ནས་བསམ་བཞིན་སེམས་ཅན་དོན་དུ་ཡེབས་
པ་ཡིན་ཕྱིར། དེས་གསུངས་པའི་བཀའ་ཆོས་དང་དེབ་རྣམས་ལ་
འབྲེལ་བ་ཐོགས་པ་ཐམས་ཅད་ལ་བྱིན་རླབས་དཔག་མེད་འབྱུང་
ངེས་པས་དད་པས་བཀླག་པར་ཞུ།
མཁན་མིང་གར་མཐར་ནས།

His Eminence, protection king, precious Traleg Kyabgon Rinpoche, having realized directly the ultimate nature of reality, Mahamudra, the great seal of truth, then chose to be born in this world to benefit all sentient beings. Those who have heard his teachings and read his books would have received immeasurable blessing with definite certainty. Hence, I urge you all to read this book with respect and faith.

Khenpo Karthar Rinpoche
Karma Triyana Dharmachakra
Woodstock New York
23 May 2018

Biography of Author
TRALEG KYABGON RINPOCHE IX

Traleg Kyabgon Rinpoche IX (1955-2012) was born in Nangchen in Kham, eastern Tibet. He was recognized by His Holiness XVI Gyalwang Karmapa as the ninth Traleg tulku and enthroned at the age of two as the supreme abbot of Thrangu Monastery. Rinpoche was taken to Rumtek Monastery in Sikkim at the age of four where he was educated with other young tulkus in exile by His Holiness Karmapa for the next five years.

Rinpoche began his studies under the auspices of His Eminence Kyabje Thuksey Rinpoche at Sangngak Choling in Darjeeling. He also studied with a number of other eminent Tibetan teachers during that time and mastered the many Tibetan teachings with the Kagyü and Nyingma traditions in particular including the *Havajra Tantra*, *Guhyasamaja Tantra*, and the third Karmapa's *Zabmo Nangdon* (*The Profound Inner Meaning*) under Khenpo Noryang (abbot of Sangngak Choling). Rinpoche studied the Abhidharmakosha, Pramanavarttika, Bodhisattvacharyavatara, *Abhidharmasamuccaya*, *Six Treaties of Nagarjuna*, the *Madhyantavibhaga*, and the *Mahayanuttaratantra* with Khenpo Sogyal. He also studied with Khenpo Sodar and was trained in tantric ritual practices by Lama Ganga, who had been specifically sent by His Holiness Karmapa for that purpose.

In 1967 Rinpoche moved to the Institute of Higher Tibetan Studies in Sarnath, and studied extensively for the next five years.

He studied Buddhist history, Sanskrit, and Hindi, as well as Longchenpa's *Finding Comfort and Ease* (*Ngalso Korsum*), *Seven Treasuries* (*Longchen Dzod Dun*), *Three Cycles of Liberation* (*Rangdrol Korsum*), and *Longchen Nyingthig* with Khenchen Palden Sherab Rinpoche and Khenpo Tsöndru.

When Rinpoche had completed these studies at the age of sixteen, he was sent by His Holiness Karmapa to study under the auspices of the Venerable Khenpo Yesha Chodar at Sanskrit University in Varanasi for three years. Rinpoche was also tutored by khenpos and geshes from all four traditions of Tibetan Buddhism during this time.

Rinpoche was subsequently put in charge of Zangdog Palri Monastery (the glorious copper colored mountain) in Eastern Bhutan and placed under the private tutelage of Dregung Khenpo Ngedon by His Holiness Karmapa to continue his studies of Sutra and Tantra. He ran this monastery for the next three years and began learning English during this time.

From 1977 to 1980, Rinpoche returned to Rumtek in Sikkim to fill the honored position of His Holiness' translator, where he dealt with many English-speaking western visitors.

Rinpoche moved to Melbourne, Australia in 1980 and commenced studies in comparative religion and philosophy at LaTrobe University. Rinpoche established E-Vam Institute in Melbourne in 1982 and went on to establish further Centers in Australia, America, and New Zealand. For the next 25 years Rinpoche gave weekly teachings, intensive weekend courses, and retreats on classic Kagyü and Nyingma texts. During this time Rinpoche also taught internationally travelling extensively through America, Europe, and South East Asia and was appointed the Spiritual Director of Kamalashila Institute in Germany for five years in the 1980's.

Rinpoche established a retreat center, Maitripa Centre in

Healesville, Australia in 1997 where he conducted two public retreats a year. Rinpoche founded E-Vam Buddhist Institute in the U.S in 2000, and Nyima Tashi Buddhist Centre in New Zealand 2004. In 2010 Rinpoche established a Buddhist college called Shogam Vidhalaya at E-Vam Institute in Australia and instructed students on a weekly basis.

Throughout his life Rinpoche gave extensive teachings on many aspects of Buddhist psychology and philosophy, as well as comparative religion, and Buddhist and western thought. He was an active writer and has many titles to his name. Titles include: the best selling *Essence of Buddhism*; *Karma, What It Is, What It Isn't, and Why It Matters*; *The Practice of Lojong*; *Moonbeams of Mahamudra*; and many more. Many of Rinpoche's books are translated in to a number of different languages including Chinese, French, German, Korean, and Spanish. Rinpoche's writings are thought provoking, challenging, profound, and highly relevant to today's world and its many challenges.

Rinpoche was active in publishing during the last two decades of his life, beginning with his quarterly magazine *Ordinary Mind* which ran from 1997 to 2003. Further, Rinpoche founded his own publishing arm Shogam Publications in 2008 and released a number of books on Buddhist history, philosophy, and psychology and left instructions for the continuation of this vision. His vision for Shogam and list of titles can be found at www.shogam.com.

Rinpoche's ecumenical approach can be seen in his other activities aimed at bringing buddhadharma to the West. He established the biannual Buddhism and Psychotherapy Conference (1994 - 2003), and Tibet Here and Now Conference (2005), and the annual Buddhist Summer School (1984 to the present).

Traleg Kyabgon Rinpoche IX passed into parinirvana on 24 July 2012, on Chokhor Duchen, the auspicious day of the Buddha's first teaching. Rinpoche stayed in meditation (*thugdam*) for weeks after his passing. A traditional cremation ceremony was conducted at Maitripa Centre and a stupa was erected on the center's grounds in Rinpoche's honor.

It is a privilege to continue to release the profound teachings of Traleg Kyabgon Rinpoche IX given in the Realized for over 30 years. Rinpoche's Sangha hope that many will benefit.

Acknowledgements

Thanks to everyone at Shogam for their help and support in producing this book. In particular, Lyn Hutchison for her editorial advice and knowledge of Tibetan; Claire Blaxell for her tireless proofing and meticulous attention to detail; Salvatore Celiento for his final proofing of the formatted book; and Felicity Lodro for her ongoing support and for creating the conditions to produce further publications of the invaluable and extensive teachings of Traleg Kyabgon Rinpoche.

I would especially like to thank Erik Pema Kunsang for his kind permission to use his translation of the root verses of *The Aspiration of the Mahamudra of True Meaning*, and Alexander Gardner, chief editor of the *Treasury of Lives* website for permission to use his biography of Rangjung Dorjé.

Finally, I would like to thank Sonam Rigzin from the Tibetan community in Australia, for providing an excellent translation of Khenpo Karthar Rinpoche's foreword.

David Bennett

Editor's Introduction

Mahamudra, *chakya chenpo* in Tibetan, literally means "great symbol" or "great seal." "*Maha*" means "great," because nothing is superior to it. "*Mudra*" means "symbol" or "seal." It is called the "great seal" or "great symbol" because Mahamudra teachings present the ultimate reality, the genuine nature of all phenomena. There is no further true meaning or true essence to discover—there is nothing to go beyond. It is the "great symbol" of reality, the actual reality of our mind, and it is the "great seal" in the same manner in which an emperor's seal speaks for the entire empire; there is nothing outside it. Mahamudra is the highest meditation training of the Sarma or new schools of Tibetan Buddhism, and a special feature of the Kagyü lineage. It represents the culmination of all the paths and stages, and the practices of the sutras and tantras.

The Mahamudra teachings are divided into three types: Sutra Mahamudra, Tantra Mahamudra, and Essence Mahamudra. Sutra Mahamudra emphasizes philosophical understanding and the meditation practices of *shamatha*[1] and vipashyana;[2] Tantra Mahamudra utilizes the Six Yogas of Naropa, tantric practices that work with subtle energies and pathways; Essence Mahamudra is based on the direct pointing-out instructions from an authentic lama and entering directly into the natural condition.

The practice and lineage of Mahamudra traces its origin back to the 8th century mahasiddha, Saraha, also known as "The Great Brahmin." Little is known of Saraha except that he was born a Brahmin but followed the Buddhist path and worked as an arrow-maker. He received tantric instruction from several Buddhist masters, observed the Brahmin laws by day and practiced the Buddhist teachings at night. He drank alcohol which eventually caused him to fall out with his fellow Brahmins and they demanded the king banish him. At an assembly in front of the king, Saraha sang three series of dohas,[3] or songs of realization—one to the king, one to the queen, and one to the people. These songs became famous as *The Three Cycles of Dohas*.

The name Saraha means "the one who has shot the arrow," and refers to one who has shot the arrow of non-duality into the heart of duality. His dohas contain the earliest Mahamudra literature and accentuate the distinctive approach of Mahamudra: the importance of pointing-out instruction from a guru, the non-dual nature of mind, "non-meditation," and "non-action," rather than reliance on more conventional spiritual practices.

In this short verse Saraha states:

> *Mind is the basis of samsara and nirvana.*
> *Once you realize its nature, rest in the ease of*
>   *non-meditation.*
> *Other than within yourself, to look for it elsewhere*
>   *is completely deluded.*
> *There is nothing of "It is this," "It is not this."*
> *Everything abides within the natural state.*

Saraha's Mahamudra lineage is known as the "long transmission lineage" of the Kagyü tradition. It begins with Saraha and goes directly to Nagarjuna, Shavaripa, Maitripa, and Marpa. The central lineage of the Kagyü tradition is the "direct transmission lineage" which includes Vajradhara, Tilopa, Naropa, and Marpa. This lineage is associated with the *anuttarayoga tantra* teachings, which are encompassed in the Six Yogas of Naropa. Saraha's principal students were Shavaripa and Nagarjuna and as is the case with

Saraha, little is known about their lives. Nagarjuna, being a disciple of Saraha who lived in the 8th century, came to be confounded with the great logician of the same name who was born in the 2nd century in south India and who founded the Madhyamaka system. This is not surprising but typical of much Indian hagiography, which was transmitted as legend rather than written down.

Shavaripa was a hunter. He was supposedly dissuaded from his livelihood by Avalokitesvara who revealed the hell realms in which Shavaripa would be reborn resulting from his actions as a hunter. Shavaripa abandoned hunting altogether and later met Saraha and Nagarjuna from whom he received Mahamudra instructions which he practiced, attaining complete realization. Shavaripa then passed these instructions on to his disciple, Maitripa.

Maitripa was originally a monk at Vikramasila monastery and was expelled by the Abbot, Atisha, when he was caught drinking alcohol and consorting with a woman during his Vajrayogini practices. After experiencing a vision of Avalokitesvara, Maitripa travelled to the south of India where he found his guru Shavaripa and received the Mahamudra practices from him. Maitripa became a very influential teacher and had many accomplished disciples, the foremost being the Tibetan, Marpa. He wrote many philosophical works on Mahamudra and is credited with rediscovering and propagating the *Mahayana-uttaratantra-shastra* of Maitreya[4] and Asanga.[5] This is the shastra which Gampopa later claimed as the doctrinal basis of Mahamudra.

Marpa (1012-1097), the great translator and yogi, was born in Lhodrak, southern Tibet. He was a householder and farmer and began studying the Dharma at an early age. He studied literary Sanskrit and the colloquial languages of India and travelled to India to study the Buddhist teachings as, at that time, Buddhism had declined in Tibet. On his first journey, Marpa became a student of the great Naropa and, on his third and final journey, he went to study with Maitripa and received the complete transmission of Saraha's Mahamudra lineage. Thus Marpa returned to Tibet holding both the "long transmission lineage" and the "direct transmission lineage" and is the originator of the Kagyü lineage in Tibet. His principal student and lineage holder was Milarepa.

Milarepa (1040-1123) was born in Gungthang province of western Tibet into a wealthy family. His father died when he was seven and his relatives took over his father's property and mistreated his family. Milarepa took revenge on them and, after meeting Marpa, went through considerable hardship in order to purify his past negative actions. He was eventually given full transmission of all Marpa's teachings and is renowned for his many years spent in isolated mountain retreats and for his spontaneous songs of realization. His student, Gampopa, became his main lineage holder.

Gampopa (1079-1153) was born into the Dakpo clan in Nyal in eastern Tibet. A doctor by profession, he was also known as Dakpo Lhaje, "the Physician from Dakpo." He was married and had two children but they, along with his wife, died during an epidemic. Before his wife died, she begged him not to marry again and to become a monk and so Gampopa became a student in the Kadam tradition which was founded in Tibet by Atisha. He attained a high level of study and learning but after overhearing a conversation about the yogi Milarepa and feeling a surge of devotion, he set out to find him, becoming his student and eventual lineage holder.

Gampopa brought together the monastic and scholastic traditions of the Kadam and the Indian Mahasiddha tradition brought to Tibet by Marpa, and was the founder of the monastic order of the Kagyü School. The lineages that branch out from him are known as the "Dakpo Kagyü." Unlike Marpa and Milarepa, Gampopa introduced Mahamudra to some of his students as a single path in itself, without the support of other practices. In Gampopa's instruction, entitled *The Single Sufficient Path of Mahamudra*, he states:

> *Mahamudra has no cause, yet faith and devotion
>   are the cause.
> Mahamudra has no condition, yet a sacred master
>   is the condition.
> Mahamudra has no method, yet non-fabrication is
>   the method.
> Mahamudra has no fruition, yet freeing concepts
>   into dharmata is the fruition.*

One of the main disciples of Gampopa and founder of the Karma Kagyü school was Dusum Khyenpa, the first Karmapa. Since then, the Karmapas have continued in an unbroken line as heads of the Karma Kagyü school and holders of the Mahamudra transmission. Rangjung Dorjé, the author of the *The Aspiration of the Mahamudra of True Meaning* is the third in the Karmapa lineage. He was born to Nyingma parents in 1284, on the eighth day of the first month of the wood-monkey year, in Tsa Pugang Zhurmo. While still a young child, his parents took him on pilgrimage in Ü[6] province in central Tibet, visiting, among other things, the famous sandalwood image of Avalokiteshvara in Kyirong. At the age of five Rangjung Dorjé received lay vows and numerous tantric initiations from Orgyenpa Rinchen Pel, (1229-1309) at his monastery of Butrasan.

According to tradition, Orgyenpa is said to have identified the youth as the reincarnation of his teacher, the second Karmapa, Karma Pakshi, and to have declared, "As my guru's esoteric name was Rangjung Dorjé, I will name you that." Other, earlier sources, however, have it that the name "Rangjung Dorjé" was given to the boy by Kunden Sherab, who gave him his novice vows. It has also been suggested that it was, in fact, Rangjung Dorjé himself who made the assertion that he was the reincarnation of Karma Pakshi.

Before his tenth birthday, Rangjung Dorjé is said to have had visions of protectors who told him to go to Tsurphu, the seat of the Karmapas. There he received teachings on various topics including Kalachakra[7] and Chö[8] from Sherap Pel, Nyenre Gendun Bum, and Namtsowa Mikyo Dorjé. At the age of eighteen, he received complete ordination from Zhonnu Jangchup, as Abbot, and Gendun Rinchen, as disciplinarian. He studied the five standard topics of a monastic curriculum:[9] *Pramana*, *Prajnaparamita*, *Madhyamaka*, *Abhidharmakosha* and *Vinaya*, with Shakya Zhonnu, an Abbot of Sangpu Monastery. He received the complete teachings of Phadampa Sangyé and Orgyenpa from Nyedo Kunga Dondrub, and instructions in the Karma Kagyü tradition from Lama Dzokden Namtso. He then went to Karma Gon in Kham, the monastery founded in 1147 by the first Karmapa, Dusum Khyenpa, and established the hermitage of Lhateng.

Back at Ü, Rangjung Dorjé donated a parasol to the Jo statue in the Jokhang, and briefly traveled to Kongpo to settle a dispute, while at Tsurphu, he constructed a temple with a gilded roof, and established the Dechen Teng hermitage at Druzhi. He continued his education, receiving Kalachakra teachings and numerous tantric initiations from Kunga Dondrup; medical instruction from Baré, Guhyasamaja and other tantric traditions from Tsultrim Rinchen; Dzogchen Nyingtik[10] from Rigdzin Kumaraja and Rikhor Repa. He went again to Kongpo, where he remained for three years, establishing the Nakpu Hermitage and several other institutions, and practiced in the mountains.

In 1326 Rangjung Dorjé returned to Ü, where he gave teachings and mediated a dispute between the Tselpa and Karma Kagyü communities. He then went east again, building an iron bridge over the Sokchu, a left-bank tributary of the Salween to the east of Karma Gön and then, going down to Kongpo, entered retreat at

Nakpu. At some point he met with Dolpopa Sherab Gyeltsen, a connection that later historians, namely Jamgon Kongtrul, used to credit Rangjung Dorjé with espousing the Shentong view.

Rangjung Dorjé returned to Ü in 1331, and that year received an invitation from the Yuan Emperor, Toq Temur, to visit the Imperial capital of Dadu, modern-day Beijing. He arrived there on November 6, 1332. Toq Temur died while the Karmapa was en route and his successor, Irinchinbal, died while the Karmapa was in the capital. He mediated a dispute over the succession, and was present when Toghan Temur was enthroned in Shangdu. While in the capital he gave the new emperor religious instruction and secured the titles "situ" and "guoshi" for his student, Kunga Dorjé, the Abbot of Tsel Gungtang. He further secured a tax exemption for Tsurphu, a remarkable set of achievements and evidence of the growing influence of the Karma Kagyü tradition in Sino-Mongolian-Tibetan affairs.

Rangjung Dorjé left China in 1334, passing through Wutai Shan, Minyak, and Markham, and arrived in Tsurphu the following year. He spent the winter of that year at Samye. Having received permission to leave China only after having promised to return in two years, not long after he had arrived in Tibet he was forced to return to China, leaving in 1336 and arriving in Dadu in 1337.

In 1338, at an assembly of officials, he is said to have declared, "I, a yogin, am like a cloud. May all those who wish to grasp the meaning of my teachings do so quickly." He passed away less than a year later, in 1339, on the fifth day of the fifth month of the rabbit year.

Although Rangjung Dorjé was of the Kagyü school he was also an important master in the Nyingma lineage. In a vision in which Vimalamitra dissolved into the place between his eyebrows, he received the teachings now known as the Karme Nyingtik and was endowed with the ability to transmit the entire Nyingtik system of

Dzogchen or Ati Yoga. He and Longchen Rabjam, one of the greatest figures in the Nyingma tradition, shared the same teacher, Rigdzin Kamaraja, and also taught each other. He composed widely on diverse topics such as doha, scriptural commentaries, astrology, Chö, and biography.

Rangjung Dorjé is said to have written *The Aspiration of the Mahamudra of True Meaning* when he went to China at the invitation of the Emperor. It conveys the meaning of Mahamudra, and encompasses the Madhyamaka, Mahamudra, and Dzogchen perspectives. It is one of several of his classic works on Mahamudra.

EDITOR'S BIOGRAPHY

David Bennett was born in Auckland, New Zealand in 1951. He developed an interest in eastern philosophical and spiritual traditions in his early twenties and encountered Buddhism in 1975 at Samye Ling, a Kagyü Tibetan Buddhist centre established by Chögyam Trungpa Rinpoche and Akong Tulku Rinpoche in Scotland in 1967. He moved to Australia in 1981 where he met Traleg Kyabgon Rinpoche IX who had recently arrived from India and had settled in Melbourne, and continued studying and practicing under his guidance until Rinpoche's untimely passing in 2012. David is a graphic designer and painter and lives in the Yarra Valley in Victoria, Australia.

SONG OF KARMAPA
The Aspiration of the
Mahamudra of True Meaning
by Lord Rangjung Dorjé

The Root Verses
Song of Karmapa

Namo guru.

All masters and yidam deities of the mandalas,
Victorious ones and spiritual sons and daughters throughout
    the three times and ten directions,
Pay heed to me and bestow your blessings
That I may attain accomplishment in accordance with my
    aspirations.

Springing forth from the snow mountain of the pure thoughts
    and deeds
Of myself and all countless beings,
May streams of virtue, undefiled by the three-fold concepts,
Flow into the ocean of the four kayas of the victorious ones.

For as long as we have not attained that,
May we, throughout our succession of lives and rebirths,
Never even hear the words "misdeeds" or "suffering,"
But enjoy this splendorous ocean of happiness and virtue.

Having obtained the supreme freedoms and riches, possessing
    faith, endeavor and intelligence,
We have followed an eminent spiritual guide and received
the nectar of oral instructions.
Without any obstacles for accomplishing them correctly,
May we, in all our lives, practice the sacred teachings.

*By learning the scriptures and through reasoning we are
    freed from the veil of ignorance.
Through contemplating the oral instructions, we overcome
    the darkness of doubt.
With the light resulting from meditation we illuminate the
    natural state as it is.
May the light of this threefold knowledge increase.*

*Through the nature of the ground, the two truths free from
    the extremes of eternalism and nihilism,
And the supreme path, the two accumulations free from the
    limits of exaggeration and denigration,
We attain the fruition of the two benefits, free from the
    extremes of existence and peace.
May we connect with such a teaching free from error.*

*The ground of purification is mind essence, the union of
    being empty and cognizant.
That which purifies is the great vajra-like practice of
    Mahamudra.
May we realize the immaculate dharmakaya—the fruition
    of having purified
All the passing stains of confusion, that are to be purified.*

*To have cut misconceptions of the ground is the confidence of
    the view.
To sustain that undistractedly is the key point of meditation.
To train in all the points of practice is the supreme action.
May we possess the confidence of view, meditation and action.*

*All phenomena are the illusory display of the mind.
Mind is devoid of "mind"—empty of any entity.
Empty and yet unceasing, it manifests as anything whatsoever.
Realizing this completely, may we cut its basis and its root.*

*We have mistaken our non-existent personal experience to
    be the objects,
And by the power of ignorance, mistaken self-cognizance to
be a 'self'.
This dualistic fixation has made us wander in the sphere of
    samsaric existence.
May we cut ignorance and confusion at the very root.*

*It is not existent since even the victorious ones do not see it.
It is not non-existent since it is the basis of samsara and
    nirvana.
This is not a contradiction, but the Middle Way of unity.
May we realize the nature of mind, free from extremes.*

*Nothing can illustrate it by the statement, "This is it."
No one can deny it by saying, "This is not it."
This nature transcending concepts is unconditioned.
May we realize this view of the true meaning.*

*Without realizing this, we circle through the ocean of
    samsara.
When realizing it, buddhahood is not somewhere else.
It is completely devoid of "it is this" or "it is not this."
May we see this vital point of the all-ground, the nature
    of things.*

*Perceiving is mind, being empty is also mind.
Realizing is mind, being mistaken is also mind.
Having arisen is mind, having ceased is also mind.
May we cut through all our doubts concerning mind.*

*Unspoiled by intellectual and deliberate meditation,
And unmoved by the winds of ordinary distractions,
May we be skilled in sustaining the practice of mind essence,
Being able to rest in unfabricated and innate naturalness.*

The waves of gross and subtle thoughts having spontaneously subsided,
The river of unwavering mind naturally abides.
Free from the stains of dullness, sluggishness and conceptualization,
May we be stable in the unmoving ocean of shamatha.

When looking again and again into the unseen mind,
The fact that there is nothing to see is vividly seen as it is.
Cutting through doubts about its nature being existent or non-existent,
May we unmistakenly recognize our own essence.

When observing objects, they are seen to be the mind, devoid of objects.
When observing the mind, there is no mind, as it is empty of an entity.
When observing both, dualistic fixation is spontaneously freed.
May we realize the natural state of the luminous mind.

Being free from mental fabrication, it is Mahamudra.
Devoid of extremes, it is the Great Middle Way.
It is also called Dzogchen, the embodiment of all.
May we attain the confidence of realizing all by knowing one nature.

Great bliss, free from attachment, is unceasing.
Luminosity, devoid of fixation, is unobscured.
Non-thought, transcending the intellect, is spontaneously present.
Without effort, may our experience be unceasing.

The fixation of clinging to good experiences is spontaneously freed.
The confusion of "bad thoughts" is naturally purified.

Ordinary mind is free from acceptance and rejection.
May we realize the truth of dharmata, devoid of constructs.

The nature of all beings is always the enlightened state.
But, not realizing it, they wander endlessly in samsara.
Towards the countless sentient beings who suffer,
May overwhelming compassion arise in our minds.

The play of overwhelming compassion being unobstructed,
In the moment of love the empty essence nakedly dawns.
May we constantly practice, day and night,
This supreme path of unity, devoid of errors.

The eyes and superknowledges resulting from the power of practice,
The ripening of sentient beings, the cultivation of buddha realms,
And the perfection of aspirations to accomplish all enlightened qualities—
May we attain the buddhahood of having accomplished ripening, cultivation and perfection.

By the power of the compassion of the victorious ones and their sons and daughters in the ten directions
And by all the perfect virtue that exists,
May I and all beings attain accomplishment in accordance with these aspirations.

This aspiration, the *Mahamudra of True Meaning*, was written by Lord Karmapa Rangjung Dorjé.[11]

Section One
The Overview

Many people have the understanding that Tibetan Buddhism, particularly in relation to the Kagyü and Nyingma schools, always has to do with some kind of visualization practice. That, however, is not true. The Mahamudra practice within the Kagyü tradition and the Dzogchen practice within the Nyingma tradition emphasize the importance of simplicity. In this way, the Mahamudra prayer by Rangjung Dorjé explains the teachings of Mahamudra in a very direct and also very simple manner.[12]

Verse 1:

All masters and yidam deities of the mandalas,
Victorious ones and spiritual sons and daughters throughout the three times and ten directions,
Pay heed to me and bestow your blessings
That I may attain accomplishment in accordance with my aspirations.

The Mahamudra prayer starts by asking the buddhas, bodhisattvas, deities, and dakinis to show compassion and love to the practitioner, so that whatever practice is engaged in is successful and bears fruit.

Verse 2:

> *Springing forth from the snow mountain of the pure*
> *   thoughts and deeds*
> *Of myself and all countless beings,*
> *May streams of virtue, undefiled by the three-fold concepts,*
> *Flow into the ocean of the four kayas of the victorious ones.*

This verse engages the practitioner in the practice of aspiration,[13] which has two aspects. The first, a general one, is contained in this verse, while the second is elaborated in the rest of the prayer.

Even though a practitioner may have the desire to attain enlightenment, this cannot be achieved purely through practicing meditation as a hermit, in isolation. Rather, it is necessary to participate in a variety of activities that bear fruit, in terms of the welfare of others. According to the imaginary Buddha in the sutra *Questions of the Naga King Anavatapta*,[14] the essence of the Buddhist teachings is the practice of compassion or, to put it another way, all the teachings come to the same point or are centralized in this notion of not abandoning sentient beings.

When "pure thoughts and deeds" are mentioned in the first line of this verse, what is meant is that the mind should be free of such things as covetousness, hurtful thoughts, and wrong views. Instead, one tries to develop love and compassion in keeping with the bodhisattva attitude. Therefore, one must desire to benefit others and so reorient one's life in the sense that instead of being self-centered, one becomes "other-centered." When the mind is put into such a mode, it does not generate the impulses that give rise to unskillful actions. This has been made clear in the text *Twenty Vows*[15] where it is said that an "other-centered" mind will never give rise to suffering for oneself.

For this reason, pure thought or motivation or intention is more important than the action. One may try to act in a moral or ethical manner, but if pure thought or motivation is absent, one's action is not skillful. It may be moral, it may be ethical, but it's not skillful. Such behavior is not fitting for someone who has embarked on the Mahayana path.

In the sutras recounting the Buddha's previous lives, it is said that in the distant past the Buddha incarnated as the captain of a ship. He saw that, out of greed, one of the crew members was intending to kill everyone on board so that he could have all the ship's riches for himself. At that time, the Buddha realized that if he, as the captain, were to kill this crew member then he would be able to save a number of lives. Killing one person, something generally considered wrong, since unethical and immoral, became skillful in that given moment. The Buddha killed the crew member and saved the lives of the others.

In Tibet there lived a very devout lama by the name of Geshé Ben who engaged in a great deal of practice. One day this geshé was informed that his benefactors would be visiting him. On hearing this, Geshé Ben thought he should organize his retreat cell properly and try to present a suitable image to his benefactors so they would continue to support him. He dusted his shrine and made everything look neat. Just before his benefactors arrived though, he realized that his intention was not pure. It occurred to him that while what he was doing may have been morally good, he did not possess pure thoughts. He immediately went to the oven and, grabbing a handful of ash, he tossed it into the air above the shrine so that it all settled on the statues, creating a mess. Upon hearing this story, Phadampa Sangyé, a great master of the Kagyü and Nyingma lineages, commented that in behaving this way the geshé had made an appropriate offering. In fact, the original offering he had arranged on the shrine, with candles, fruit, and various items placed in front of the statues, was nothing compared to the ash he threw at the statues, the reason for this being that the throwing of the ash was done with pure thought.

The above story illustrates how one's intention or motivation has to be pure. Having developed pure thought or intention or motivation then that should manifest in deed or action; as it says in the text, "pure thoughts and deeds." When the pure thought or motivation is present then it must be expressed and the way in which it is expressed is through physical means, mainly bodily movements and verbalization; they must go together. The thought and deed, or thought and action, or intention and action, are compared to the snow mountain. The text says, "Springing forth from the snow mountain of pure thoughts and deeds…" When one is not completely obsessed with the idea of morality but has the idea of skillful means in mind, realizing the importance of motivation and intention rather than action then one is able to see that the action must follow from the intention, rather than the other way around. All that one does can be compared to the stream which emanates from the melting of the snow. Through the meeting of these two, the intention and the action, one produces varieties of karmic imprints that are the streams that flow from the snow mountain. The snow mountain is the metaphor for the co-incidence of thought and action.

Another point that should be made in this context is that if one has embarked on the Mahayana path and is concerned about one's actions or one's motivation or intention, one should rid oneself of thoughts concerned with the object that may be affected by one's action, the action itself, and the agent. This means that the object, either a person or an inanimate object, the action, and the agent that brings the action into effect, are interdependent. As things do not exist as discrete entities having self-sufficient existence, but instead are interdependent, the practitioner of Mahayana does not entertain such thoughts. For this reason, the mind of such a practitioner is devoid of these pollutants.

Chandrakirti[16] commented in *Entering the Middle Way*[17], that even while one engages in prayer, if one's mind is not free from this "three-term relationship"—the object of prayer, the act of praying, and the agent who prays—then one still remains in samsara or the world of cyclic existence. This is because one sees the object of prayer, the act of praying, and the agent as being distinct and existing independently of each other. However, if one does not involve oneself with such thoughts then one attains enlightenment. An action free of the three-term relationship is not an ordinary action. It's called an "action of the *paramita*" or "transcendental action." An action performed with thoughts of the independence of object, the act, and the subject or agent is, on the other hand, a "non-paramita action."

We could say the same thing in relation to the practice of all six paramitas[18] in Buddhism. Take, for example, the paramita or transcendental action of generosity. If a person practicing generosity does something generous and thoughts of the object, act, and agent arise, then that is not the paramita of generosity. However, when such thoughts are absent and one realizes the interdependence of this three-term relationship, then that act of generosity becomes a paramita. Therefore, the follower of the Mahayana tries to understand that the intention is more important than the action. Even in terms of an action, understanding its relativity is important, because to understand that is to understand how wisdom and compassion—which is synonymous with skillful means—are interrelated. Without an understanding of the three-term relationship, actions lack wisdom.

One must also appreciate the interdependence of wisdom and compassion or "skill-in-means." Wisdom that is developed mainly through meditation could become contrived. As a result of a lack of compassion, practitioners can become excessively contemplative and oriented towards liberation or enlightenment. On the other hand, if practitioners are only concerned with the development of compassion and applying skill-in-means in their lives without cultivating wisdom, they remain in cyclic existence and do not achieve enlightenment. Skill-in-means relates to one's action whereas wisdom relates to the mind that understands that the practitioner's action is also relative, not something absolute. Wisdom involves the practitioner's understanding of emptiness, which means seeing things in terms of relationship rather than essence and substance. Wisdom divorced from skill-in-means binds the practitioner to nirvana, while skill-in-means divorced from wisdom binds the practitioner to samsara.

So that is what is meant by, "May streams of virtue, undefiled by the three-fold concepts, flow into the ocean of the four kayas of the victorious ones." The "three-fold concepts" refer to the misconception of an independent object, act, and agent. Virtue is developed from an understanding of this three-term relationship. This can then become a seed for the realization of the three aspects of buddha's being: the *nirmanakaya* or manifest being, the *sambhogakaya* or symbolic aspect of buddha's being, and the *dharmakaya* or authentic aspect of buddha's being. The verse mentions four "kayas," the fourth being the *svabhavikakaya*, the unitive aspect of buddha's being.

The dharmakaya, or authentic aspect of buddha's being, refers to the nature of the mind itself. Dharmakaya is seen as the source from which the practitioner's own self-interest is realized, while the interests of others are accomplished through the sambhogakaya and nirmanakaya. Dharmakaya is the source from which the other attributes of enlightenment arise. The other aspects of buddha's being are a result of these attributes but dharmakaya, or the authentic state of buddha's being, in itself, is without attributes. It is a state of being which is completely open and therefore indeterminate; it is devoid of characteristics and attributes. It is compared to space itself because it is due to space that everything exists. Without space, nothing would exist, but space does not have definable characteristics, as do concrete physical objects.

The sambhogakaya, or symbolic aspect of buddha's being, refers to the symbolic manifestations of the enlightened qualities. These can arise in the form of visions or dreams. Although these images have definable characteristics, they do not have physical existence. While on the path, practitioners may be subject to many types of visionary experiences, all emanating from the domain of sambhogakaya or the symbolic aspect of being.

Then there is the nirmanakaya, the physical aspect of buddha's being, which is physically tangible and perceptible to the senses. These three aspects of buddha's being are normally called the three *kayas, trikaya* in Sanskrit. Kaya is normally translated as "body" and these three aspects exist as a unity; the three kayas do not exist independent of each other. This is borne out by the notion of svabhavikakaya, or the unitive aspect of buddha's being. Sometimes translators call the unitive aspect of buddha's being, "body of great bliss." It refers to the totality of being enlightened. The four kayas, or four aspects of buddha's being, are referred to as "the ocean" in the prayer: "...flow into the ocean of the four kayas of the victorious ones." The "victorious ones" refers to the buddhas. When thoughts and deeds coincide, they are like the snow mountain, and all the virtuous, positive qualities that one might develop from then on are compared to the streams flowing from the snow mountains which then merge into the ocean. These are the four qualities or four aspects of buddha's being. Jamgön Kongtrul Rinpoche[19] says that where certain physical images are used in Indian and Tibetan poetry to describe different types of qualities of the mind then this is termed "the use of metaphor."

Section Two

The Correct Basis for Embarking on the Path

We have discussed the first two verses of the prayer. With the second verse, the core theme of the prayer is laid out. It covers the basis, path, and fruition of the practitioner's spiritual progress.

Commencing with the third verse, the prayer is divided into sections. The first section is concerned with the necessity of having a correct spiritual and physical basis to embark on the path and the prayer is directed towards realizing that possibility. Insight is essential to make progress on the path and the second section of the text is devoted to the prayer which makes it possible for the practitioner to develop correct understanding through insight. Then, because the path should be devoid of errors, the third section of the prayer is directed towards the path itself. The fourth section of the text is devoted to a prayer that enables the practitioner to apply various spiritual methods, so that the path is incorporated within one's being. The last section of the Mahamudra prayer is directed towards fruition of the spiritual quest.

Verse 3

> *For as long as we have not attained that,*
> *May we, throughout our succession of lives and rebirths,*
> *Never even hear the words "misdeeds" or "suffering,"*
> *But enjoy this splendorous ocean of happiness and virtue.*

As has been pointed out, this verse is a prayer for the appropriate physical and spiritual basis to embark on the spiritual path. It starts with, "For as long as we have not attained that…" Here, "that" refers to the state of enlightenment. The state of enlightenment is the embodiment of the four aspects of buddha's being mentioned in the second verse. These four aspects of buddha's being possess the dual qualities of compassion and wisdom. The physical aspect of buddha's being results from having actualized the potentialities of compassion and wisdom. Wisdom is realized through the mental aspect of buddha's being. This wisdom has two aspects, *jitawa* and *jinyepa* in Tibetan. *Jitawa* is the wisdom that apprehends the nature of things; the wisdom that enables the buddha to apprehend ultimate reality. *Jinyepa* is the wisdom that enables the buddha to perceive the extent of things, empirical reality. These two aspects or kinds of wisdom enable the enlightened being, the buddha, to apprehend the dual aspects of reality normally referred to as "ultimate truth" and "relative truth." The buddha has the ability to apprehend both levels of reality simultaneously, due to the penetrating insight of this full-blown wisdom.

The second part of the verse deals with the samsaric condition. Prior to realizing the four aspects of buddha's being, the practitioner is an ordinary sentient being and so is pushed and pulled by the mechanism of causality, or cause and effect. The prayer thus makes an aspiration that, until the four aspects of buddha's being are realized, the practitioner remains free of both the cause and the experience of suffering. This is referred to in the phrase, "never even hear the words 'misdeeds' or 'suffering'".

To explain this further, the direct result of engaging in unskillful actions will be the experience of suffering. So instead of becoming entangled in the confusion of unwholesome actions, the prayer inspires the practitioner towards having the wisdom to choose actions that are beneficial. Such actions are of benefit to oneself.

They are the cause of happiness rather than suffering. The prayer then goes on to state: "But enjoy this splendorous ocean of happiness and virtue." To put this in other words, it is an aspiration that the practitioner may experience a perpetual sense of wellbeing and happiness.

In order to determine what sorts of actions are non-beneficial, the text, *Precious Garland*[20] explains:

> All actions stemming from negative or deluded states of mind, states of mind corrupted by hate, grasping or ignorance are always unskillful and non-beneficial. They cannot be anything other than the potential cause of one's experience of suffering and misery. Actions that originate from states of mind devoid of these pollutants should be judged as being beneficial and wholesome. These actions are necessary and sufficient conditions for one to enjoy a sense of wellbeing and to experience happiness.

Entering into the Conduct of a Bodhisattva[21] also makes the same point. It exhorts the practitioner to be forever vigilant, both day and night, with respect to their thoughts and actions, and by understanding the causal relationship between one's deeds and one's experiences.

Verse 4

> *Having obtained the supreme freedoms and riches,*
>   *possessing faith, endeavor and intelligence,*
> *We have followed an eminent spiritual guide and received*
>   *the nectar of oral instructions.*
> *Without any obstacles for accomplishing them correctly,*
> *May we, in all our lives, practice the sacred teachings.*

Before embarking on the spiritual path, the practitioner must ensure that they possess the necessary physical and spiritual attributes. Physically, not only does one need a human body, but that body should be free of certain physical defects and impediments. These defects and impediments refer to physical and mental incapacity that prevents practicing and understanding the Dharma. One must also possess certain qualities, such as having a caring attitude towards others and being compassionate and altruistic. The human body then should be free of both physical and psychological impairment and also endowed with the requisite physical and mental faculties. Without these, one cannot establish the spiritual basis. When the verse mentions "freedoms," this means being free of significant physical and mental obstacles, while "riches" refers to having the physical and mental faculties sufficiently intact.

The spiritual basis consists of having "faith" (Tib. *depa*); "endeavor" or "vigor," sometimes translated as "effort" (Tib. *tsöndru*); and "intelligence" or "insight" (Tib. *sherap*). Having the correct basis for one's spiritual development involves ensuring all of these are present.

There are four different types of faith in this context: admiration, strong interest, trusting faith, and unshakeable confidence. In Tibetan, admiration is *döpai depa*. *Dopa* normally means "interest" or "inclination." This type of faith is developed through having an interest in spiritual matters or having the inclination to develop a further understanding of them.

The second is called "strong interest," "longing," or "yearning," *dangway depa* in Tibetan. Dangway depa is based on the first faith, döpai depa. Having developed a certain interest in spiritual matters, the practitioner has a limited form of confidence in the validity of the teachings as well as in the practice. This type of faith arises when the trust is deepened. Dangwa literally means "lucid" or "clear." The practitioner has less resistance towards practice and their confidence increases. As an outcome of practice, the mind may become more settled, more focused, and therefore less turbulent. As a result, the practitioner is able to more clearly perceive the teachings and the spiritual practice.

The third type of faith is called *yichepai depa* in Tibetan, and is a further growth from the two preceding types of faith. *Yichepa* literally means "conviction." Here, the practitioner's faith of conviction is developed through experience in practice. This development of faith then culminates in what is called *michepai depa* in Tibetan, which literally means "incontrovertible" faith. This faith has less to do with confidence or faith as we normally understand it, and more to do with the direct experience of the nature of reality itself. Having had direct experience of reality, the practitioner's experience is no longer feeble or fickle. It does not fluctuate and is therefore called "incontrovertible faith."

The first three stages of faith can co-exist with doubts and uncertainties. Even a persistent confidence or faith in the teachings and practice may be disturbed by the intermittent arousal of doubt and uncertainty. These first three forms of faith are therefore not totally stable. This is particularly so with the first two. Nevertheless, through greater understanding of the teachings and deeper familiarity and appreciation of the practice, the practitioner's faith can deepen and be converted into "incontrovertible faith."

While cultivating faith, one should also develop vigor. The continuous application of vigor in spiritual practice prevents a practitioner from yielding to laziness and various distractions, and from indulging in apathy. Through the application of vigor, practitioners are able to sustain their interest in the teachings and the practice. The last element of the spiritual basis is the development of insight. Even if faith is present and vigor applied, the mind may not be lucid. As a result of this, the mind is devoid of insight, and so one of the constituents of the spiritual basis of the path is missing.

When these three spiritual elements are present, one should seek a spiritual guide or friend, known as *gewai shenyen* in Tibetan. *Gewa* means "all that is wholesome," *shenyen* means "friend." This refers to a friend who is able to instruct and help one along the path. The verse expresses this with the line, "We have followed an eminent spiritual guide and received the nectar of oral instructions."

Not only should the teacher have the necessary qualities, they should also be able to impart their instructions without distortion. In this particular context, these are the spiritual instructions with regard to the relationship between the three vehicles, the Hinayana, Mahayana, and Vajrayana, or the instructions comprising the triple training: training in morality, training in meditation, and training in insight. The teacher's instruction may also relate to the Mahayana concepts of interpretive and definitive teachings. The teacher should have the ability to identify and differentiate two types of sutras: those containing only relative teachings and those that contain teachings definitive in their meaning. Relative teachings are not definitive in content and require interpretation; they should not be taken too literally. Definitive teachings, on the other hand, should not be interpreted and so are to be taken fairly literally.

The teacher should also have the ability to put the teachings in context. In looking at a particular text or sutra, for example, the teacher must have an understanding of who the audience was at the time, who the sutra was addressed to, in what context, and with what intention. Simply understanding the words in a given sutra is not sufficient. This ability is compared to nectar, that mythical substance which grants immortality to anyone taking a sip, and is considered the essence of liberation. If this ability is lacking, distortions will be introduced into the teachings. This will then affect whoever tries to practice them.

Having received the appropriate spiritual instructions from a teacher in possession of the necessary qualities, to whatever extent, the practitioner should not simply leave it at that. They must practice accordingly. As the verse says, "Without any obstacles for accomplishing them correctly, may we, in all our lives, practice the sacred teachings." Practitioners must practice the teachings, otherwise their practice will suffer from interruptions and disruptions. The verse then concludes with the aspiration to be successful in the unerring accomplishment of the teachings.

Section Three

The Means of Realizing the Path

The previous two verses concentrated on the importance of obtaining an environment conducive to practicing the Dharma. This environment includes being of sufficiently sound mind and body, being inclined towards spirituality as a whole, and having sought a teacher with the ability to provide the instructions and guidance necessary for one's spiritual practice. Once one has established the appropriate conditions and environment, to have simply decided to embark on the path is not enough, because the path has to be fully understood. For that to occur, one must develop wisdom or insight. The following verse is connected to the development of wisdom on the path:

Verse 5

By learning the scriptures and through reasoning we are freed from the veil of ignorance.
Through contemplating the oral instructions we overcome the darkness of doubt.
With the light resulting from meditation we illuminate the natural state as it is.
May the light of this threefold knowledge increase.

The first line emphasizes the importance of hearing and studying the teachings. The second highlights the need to contemplate those teachings. It is not sufficient to simply hear and study the teachings;

one has to properly assimilate them. The third line refers to the third means of accessing knowledge, which is meditation. Having heard, studied, and contemplated the teachings, one must engage in the practice of meditation so that the mediated and conceptual understanding and knowledge can be translated into direct experience. The fourth line makes mention of "the light" of this threefold knowledge. In other words, this is an aspiration that these three forms of knowledge give rise to an understanding of ultimate reality, or the nature of things.

Returning to the first line, here the scriptures are specifically mentioned. In the canonical teachings of Buddhism the scriptures have two components. The first consists of the oral discourses of the Buddha, *ka* in Tibetan. The second is the commentarial material, *tenchö* in Tibetan, which explicates different points raised by the Buddha in his discourses. Not all of the discourses included in the first type of material, the ka, were actually spoken by the Buddha; the Buddha may have used someone else to speak on his behalf. So because the Buddha had granted permission to somebody else to speak on his behalf, this material is included as part of the oral teachings.

The subject matter of the oral discourses and commentarial material is organized into three divisions. The first has to do with the Vinaya teachings. These teachings generally cover moral and ethical matters, including the enumeration of vows or precepts. The second consists of teachings that deal with a variety of metaphysical issues. These include discussions on the relationship between relative and ultimate truth as presented in the sutras. The last section is the Abhidharma. These are the teachings designed to elucidate the material found in the sutras and give more detail. The Abhidharma is a systematized presentation of the material based on the different categories it falls into. These categories include such things as mind and matter. While there are many kinds of teachings, both within the oral discourses themselves and the commentarial material, all are subsumed under these three divisions.

In terms of the cultivation of the first means of knowledge, although one needs to hear and study the teachings, one should not pursue one's study in a non-reflective manner. In other words, the teachings should neither be accepted at face value nor should one's acceptance of the teachings be based only on faith; one should engage in reasoning. As the third Karmapa points out, "By learning the scriptures and through reasoning we are freed from the veil of ignorance." One should study the Vinaya, the Sutras, and Abhidharma material in the form of both original discourse and the commentarial literature, but one should do so through the use of valid reasoning. When one discovers that the material studied does not violate the rules of reasoning or logic, then one has to accept it as valid.

It is by combining learning with reasoning that one develops the wisdom or insight that arises from hearing and studying, referred to as *thöjung gi sherap* in Tibetan. Through the development of this first type of wisdom or insight, it is said that one is able to dispel "the clouds of unknowing". The lack of understanding or ignorance referred to here is on the ordinary level; it means not being properly informed. It is through this first type of wisdom that misunderstandings, distortions, and a total lack of understanding are dispelled. According to Chandrakirti:

> An individual who has developed sufficient understanding through learning, who also has acumen, should be compared to someone with sight. One person with sight can lead many others who are blind to their desired destination.

Learning should thus complement one's logical acumen, and one's ability to reason should complement one's learning and scholarship; they should not be separated.

As the second line of the verse explains: "through contemplating the oral instructions we overcome the darkness of doubt." So through the cultivation of contemplation, which is the second means to obtain insight, one contemplates on the oral instructions, called *mengak* in Tibetan, *upadesa* in Sanskrit. When one studies a text, the teacher may provide instructions on how to understand certain delicate points that have been made and how those points relate to one's own experience. In this way, the discussions do not remain purely on the level of abstraction but are on the concrete level of matching one's intellectual understanding with the psychological and spiritual processes going on within the practitioner. By assimilating the teachings into one's being, the discussions which have arisen in the course of study are not left completely on the intellectual level of total detachment but are brought alive by matching the concepts discussed in the text with one's own experience.

Contemplating in that way brings about the second type of insight, *samjung gi sherap* in Tibetan; *sam* means "contemplation" and *sherap* means "insight." In the previous case, one became more informed about the various spiritual matters discussed by the Buddha or subsequent teachers and commentators. One was thus broadening understanding and dispelling the clouds of unknowing. In this particular case, however, when insight arises due to contemplation, conviction also arises and eradicates one's doubts. It's not just a case of increasing intellectual understanding, but of having more confidence in what one is doing and in one's own understanding. This confidence arises as a result of contemplation and being able to match the concepts discussed in the text with one's experience.

The text states: "Through contemplating the oral instructions we overcome the darkness of doubt. With the light resulting from meditation, we illuminate the natural state as it is." To summarize, firstly practitioners try to increase their learning, sharpen their intellect, and have some experiential understanding, so that the teachings do not remain on the level of abstraction, are assimilated on a personal level, and a certain amount of confidence develops.

Then one must practice meditation, which is the third means of attaining insight, *gomjung gi sherap* in Tibetan. *Gom* means "meditation," *jung* means "arising from," and *sherap* means "insight" or "wisdom." Putting all this together, gomjung gi sherap means "insight arising from the practice of meditation." In the first case one became more informed and developed greater intellectual appreciation. In the second case one developed more confidence. Then, unlike the previous two, in the third case, through the practice of meditation that is the culmination of the development of insight, one not only has confidence but gains insight into the natural state of everything that exists. One has direct perception of ultimate reality, also known as suchness or *tathata*.

There is an expression found in the teachings—"from *rupa* to nirvana." *Rupa* means "matter" or "form" in Sanskrit and nirvana of course, means "enlightenment." This is basically saying that between these two everything is included; nothing is left out. One gains insight into the nature of how the world exists and insight into the nature of the body and the nature of the mind because one realizes that one's own ordinary body is the embodiment of the physical aspect of buddha's being. This is sometimes referred to as "body of great bliss," and is a translation of the Tibetan term *dewa chenpo zuk*; *dewa* means "bliss," *chenpo* means "great," and *zuk* means "body," so all together it means "the body of great bliss."

This very body is the basis of the enlightened mind. In its authentic condition, its non-corrupted form, it coexists in harmony with the nature of the mind. The nature of the mind is unlike the mind that is active in the normal context. It is completely free of any kind of restriction, completely open like the authentic dimension of the body. The nature of the mind in its natural condition is devoid of delusions and other pollutants. Such insight is made possible due to the practice of meditation where one has direct experience of the nature of things and the nature of one's being, in its physical and mental aspects.

In the teachings it is said that such harmonious coexistence of the physical and mental aspects of one's being is like ice and water. In reality, one cannot differentiate one from the other. Such insight is obtained only through the practice of meditation, not through contemplation or learning and reasoning. However, those two can be helpful in leading the practitioner along the right path. Through the practice of meditation one is able to gain direct insight into the nature of things, the nature of all that exists. The text thus states: "With the light resulting from meditation we illuminate the natural state as it is." The light that results from the practice of meditation can illuminate or shed light on ultimate reality.

According to the teachings, for most of us, unless we already have superior understanding, this is the order in which we should be approaching the path. First, we should try to develop intellectual understanding through learning and improving our logical acumen. Then we should try to go beyond that by translating learning into personal understanding of what these things mean. Eventually we must practice meditation so that we have immediate rather than mediated insight. Through these three different types of insight or wisdom, we are able to have some understanding of the spiritual path. We may have been able to obtain a conducive environment and possess the right kinds of conditions to embark on the spiritual path, but if we do not have an understanding of the path we are following then it is very difficult to make progress. Therefore, right from the beginning, we must understand that insight is extremely important and we must know how it is cultivated.

The 3rd Karmapa concludes the verse by saying, "May the practitioner be able to develop these three types of insight so that correct understanding of the path will arise."

Section Four

The Path

Having dealt with the means of realizing the path, the next verse has to do with the path itself:

Verse 6

*Through the nature of the ground, the two truths free from
  the extremes of eternalism and nihilism,
And the supreme path, the two accumulations free from
  the limits of exaggeration and denigration,
We attain the fruition of the two benefits, free from the
  extremes of existence and peace.
May we connect with such a teaching free from error.*

The first line describes the ground of being or ultimate reality that has to be realized. The second points out the methods involved in realizing this. The third line of the verse talks about the importance of not indulging in extremes, in terms of actions. The fourth requests that the practitioner be fortunate enough to meet with teachings that possess certain qualities and are without error. These qualities are that they (a) have the ability to lead the practitioner to realization of the ground of being or ultimate reality, (b) help the practitioner be discerning when it comes to the methods involved in achieving that goal, and (c) put the practitioner in possession of wisdom so that their actions are not corrupted as a result of having a distorted understanding of ultimate reality.

Ultimate reality itself, which is the ground of being and the source from which everything that exists arises, has to be properly understood. One therefore needs to develop the correct view. This can be achieved only if the practitioner avoids the temptation to interpret ultimate reality either from the point of view of eternalism or from the point of view of nihilism. The eternalist view asserts that everything exists in an ultimate sense and so has some kind of enduring essence or substance. The nihilistic view claims that things have no real existence whatsoever.

According to the Mahayana teachings, certain religions and philosophies fall into such distorted ways of understanding or interpreting ultimate reality. Many theistic religions posit all kinds of permanent, incontrovertible, absolute entities such as the concept of God or the immortality of the soul. On the other hand, by entertaining a nihilistic view, some people have even come to deny the legitimacy or existence of moral principles. They take the stance that if nothing exists fundamentally then there is no meaning and no such thing as moral principles that one can appeal to.

If one is to understand the ground of being, which is ultimate reality and in fact a synonym for the word "Mahamudra," then one should adopt the middle view. This middle view does not have the inherent problems associated with the extreme views of eternalism or nihilism. It is important to adopt the middle view and avoid the two extreme views because that is how ultimate reality itself exists. Ultimate reality cannot be said to exist in the conventional sense and, at the same time, one cannot say that it does not exist at all. So, "The two truths, free from the extremes of eternalism and nihilism," means that ultimate reality exists where relative truth and ultimate truth co-exist in harmony, in unity.

From the point of view of ultimate truth, reality has no enduring essence or substance so therefore does not have inherent existence. From the point of view of relative truth, however, things have conventional existence; things come into being due to the interaction of causes and conditions. Ultimate truth is the aspect of reality as-it-is in itself, its existential aspect. Reality as-it-is in itself is free from all kinds of determinate characteristics and is therefore often compared to space. Since reality in its existential condition is something devoid of attributes, qualities, or characteristics, then no words can be formed to describe it. Terms such as "ground of being," "emptiness," "primordial reality," and "absolute truth" are, however, used to refer to the aspect of reality as-it-exists in itself.

The concept of relative truth brings out the phenomenal aspect of that reality or, in other words, the way in which reality appears to the conscious mind. In its phenomenal aspect, things come into being due to causes and conditions and therefore things do exist on the conventional level. They do so because of *pratityasamutpada*, which means "dependent arising" or "dependent origination." If practitioners are able to understand how ultimate and relative truth co-exist in harmony, in unity, and without conflict, they can resist the illusions of the extreme views of eternalism and nihilism. Even though things do not have enduring essence or substance in the *way* they exist, when viewed from the point of view of *how* they exist in their actual condition, it can be seen that phenomena, which are products of causes and conditions, arise from that emptiness.

Nihilism is avoided with the concept of relative truth and eternalism is avoided with the notion of absolute truth. For this reason, Nagarjuna[22] has stated that wherever emptiness is possible, everything is possible. Where emptiness is not possible, however, then nothing is possible. Ultimate truth and relative truth cannot be separated; they co-exist . It is because of emptiness that things can exist in the first place. Without emptiness, as Nagarjuna has pointed out, nothing could exist at all. Therefore, when it is not understood correctly and not perceived in terms of its relationship with ultimate truth, relative truth itself is mistakenly conceived to have enduring essence. This misunderstanding arises in ordinary human beings. Even though things come into being due to causes and conditions, nevertheless, because of the delusions of the mind, things are thought to have some kind of essence that is immutable, unchanging, and permanent. However, the *aryas*, or spiritually developed beings, are able to perceive how relative truth and ultimate truth co-exist. As a result of having realized ultimate truth, such individuals do not dwell on thoughts of substance and essence.

In this way, one should not underestimate relative truth or phenomena by saying that it is all illusory and has no significance. On the contrary, it is due to gaining insight into relative truth that one is able to realize absolute truth. At the same time, one has to see the importance of understanding ultimate truth as well. Without an understanding of ultimate truth, enlightenment is not possible. For this reason, one has to pay equal attention to the two aspects of the reality: reality viewed as existing as-it-is in itself, and reality viewed from the aspect of phenomena.

While the first line of the verse elaborates on the importance of gaining insight into ultimate reality, with the knowledge or cognitive aspect, the second deals with the moral dimension. If practitioners have been able to cultivate the correct view as described in the first line, then they would have the discernment to avoid being corrupted on the level of morality. However, if that view is not attained, then certain moral embellishments may take place. This occurs in two different ways.

Firstly, the practitioner may place too much emphasis on the reality of moral principles and therefore exaggerate their import. If moral principles are interpreted as having enduring essence or substance—in other words, if they are seen as absolutes—then that is a form of exaggeration, because more importance is given to moral principles than they actually have.

Alternatively, it may be thought that from the ultimate point of view, since nothing has enduring essence or substance and everything is emptiness, then nothing matters and therefore "anything goes." If the relevance of moral principles is denied altogether, and one is seen to be free to do whatever one feels like doing without regard for morality, then that leads to the other extreme, the extreme of denigration.

So, in terms of one's knowledge of the ground of being or reality, one should avoid the two extreme views of eternalism and nihilism and, in terms of one's actions, one should avoid the extremes of exaggeration and denigration.

When that is understood, the practitioner should strive towards achieving enlightenment with the practice of the two accumulations—the accumulation of merit and the accumulation of wisdom. The accumulation of merit is achieved through the practice of compassion and other religious observances. The accumulation of wisdom is cultivated through hearing, contemplating, and meditating, the three means of attaining wisdom. In terms of the means of achieving enlightenment, the practitioner also has to be vigilant not to fall into extreme behavior. For example, it is possible to focus too much on wisdom and meditation and withdraw into oneself. In doing so, one does not pay attention to the aspect of being in the world, of being with others. If the aspect of compassion is either not practiced fully or is ignored altogether, then another form of imbalance arises. The same thing can be said of a practitioner who is too concerned about the suffering, injustice, and inequality that afflicts living creatures. Through being totally moved by the prevalence of suffering and forgetting to engage in contemplation or meditation and the development of wisdom then, again, the practitioner suffers. It is therefore essential to pay equal attention to the practice of compassion, which creates merit, and the practice of contemplation and meditation, that gives rise to wisdom.

Generally speaking, one should try to practice the six paramitas, also known as the "six transcendental actions." When the two accumulations are pursued with equal zeal and enthusiasm then the direct result is realization of the two aspects of buddha's being, namely the physical aspect and the mental aspect. The verse says, "We attain the fruition of the two benefits, free from the extremes of existence and peace." The "two benefits" refer to the benefit to oneself and the benefit to others. Realization of the mental aspect of buddha's being, which is the product of wisdom, fulfils the practitioner's benefit because it leads to realization of their own authentic nature. The accumulation of merit results in actualization of the physical aspect of buddha's being, which has the capacity to benefit others through use of the body, both physically and verbally. Therefore, the enlightened being has the capacity to alleviate others' suffering and distress. Atisha,[23] for example, in his *Lamp of Enlightenment*[24] has devoted many pages to extolling the virtues of practicing the two accumulations with equal amounts of zeal and enthusiasm.

The third line is, "We attain the fruition of the two benefits, free from the extremes of existence and peace." When enlightenment has been achieved, the buddha neither remains in this world nor exclusively in the state of nirvana. The buddha does not exclusively remain in the state of nirvana because of the power of compassion. The state of nirvana may be peaceful but, nevertheless, due to the overwhelming amount of suffering and pain endured by ordinary sentient beings, the buddha or enlightened being does not indulge in that peaceful state of nirvana. Because of wisdom, the enlightened being does not dwell in samsara, for although the buddha may be able to experience and perceive others' suffering, nevertheless the enlightened being cannot be perturbed by the goings-on in samsara. The simple reason is that the enlightened being has eradicated delusion and conceptual confusion, the cause of mental disturbance. So, due to the mental aspect of buddha's being or dharmakaya, the buddha does not remain in samsara and, because of the physical embodiment, the buddha does not remain in the state of nirvana or peace.

This verse, as a whole, brings out the importance of not falling into extremes. In terms of knowledge with respect to ultimate reality, the practitioner should avoid falling into the extremes of eternalism and nihilism. In terms of moral practice, the practitioner should try to avoid the extremes of exaggeration and denigration. In terms of fruition, the buddha or enlightened being avoids the extremes of both the samsaric condition, which is full of dissatisfaction, anxiety, and distress, and the complete quietude and peace of nirvana.

The verse basically points out the importance of understanding this in relation to what is called *shi* in Tibetan, *alaya* in Sanskrit, or "the ground of being." This is the starting point, the path, and the fruition. The ground of being has two aspects, relative truth and ultimate truth. In terms of the path, it again has two aspects, wisdom and compassion. Finally, in terms of fruition it also has two aspects, the physical and mental aspects of buddha's being. As a practitioner, one has to form a non-erroneous view with respect to the ground of being, reality. In order to develop this understanding, one needs to engage in the practice of the two accumulations of merit and wisdom to avoid the extremes of exaggeration and denigration. When one has become freed from these constraints then one is able to attain buddhahood or enlightenment, which does not fall into the extremes of either samsara or nirvana.

The last line of the verse is, "May we connect with such a teaching free from error." The verse concludes with the prayer to have the good fortune to encounter a teacher who possesses these capabilities, in terms of dealing with the ground, path, and fruition.

Section Five

How to Cultivate the Spiritual Path

We now come to the section of the prayer in which the method used to cultivate the spiritual path is elucidated. The seventh verse presents the essence or gist of the verses to follow, all of which concern the cultivation of Mahamudra practice.

There are several issues addressed in this verse. First of all, before one gets to the specifics of Mahamudra meditation practice, one has to develop an understanding of the basis of the spiritual purification to be conducted. Secondly, one develops an understanding of the method to be used to accomplish one's goal. Thirdly, what it is that has been purified is looked at. Finally the result of purification is addressed.

Verse 7

> *The ground of purification is mind essence , the union of being empty and cognizant.*
> *That which purifies is the great vajra-like practice of Mahamudra.*
> *May we realize the immaculate dharmakaya—the fruition of having purified*
> *All the passing stains of confusion that are to be purified.*

The first line of the verse is concerned with elucidating the basis for purification, the mind essence, or the nature of the mind. The second line explains the method of purification, the practice of Mahamudra. In the Tibetan stanzas of the verse, the object of purification is mentioned next.[25] What is being purified are the passing stains, or "adventitious defilements," which are said to arise from five sources: clinging, hostility, laziness, mental agitation, and doubt or extreme skepticism. They are called "adventitious" because they are temporary. Defilements associated with the deluded mind are temporary in the sense that they are removable. The way in which these delusions have come into being and how they arise in the mind is discussed later in the text, so there's no need to elaborate on that at present. The verse finishes with a comment on the result of the purification that has been achieved.

The basis

There are numerous obstacles and delusions to be overcome on the spiritual path. The practitioner needs to recognize the basis for purification, however, which is the nature of the mind itself. The nature of the mind has to be distinguished from mind or consciousness as it is understood in a conventional sense. The nature of the mind is intrinsically pure and has two characteristics, emptiness and luminosity. The practitioner must realize that what needs to be purified is not the nature of the mind as such, in its absolute aspect, because the nature of the mind has been pure right from the beginning. As it is intrinsically pure, it is not vulnerable to corruption. According to Mahamudra teachings, it has to be understood that what needs to be purified are temporary delusions or adventitious defilements. To reiterate this point, the practitioner needs to understand the nature of the mind is the *basis* for purification but not the object of purification. If one does not understand this, one does not understand the Mahamudra view.

Because of this, the nature of the mind has to be distinguished from one's conventional understanding of the mind—the empirical mind which has thoughts, which remembers, which wills, intends, and so forth. The portion of the mind referred to as "the nature of the mind" is pure whereas the portion of the mind that relates to one's everyday experience is impure. In the Mahamudra teachings, empirical consciousness is referred to as "impure consciousness" or "deluded mind," while the nature of the mind is called "immaculate mind." The nature of the mind possesses the two characteristics of being empty of all kinds of determinate characteristics, on the one hand, and being cognizant or luminous, on the other. Even though one experiences thoughts, ideas, and emotions arising and subsiding in the mind, from the point of view of the immaculate mind or the nature of the mind, there is no such activity occurring. It is completely free of any notion of birth and death, coming into being or going out of existence, precisely because it is empty. It is not vulnerable to attacks of delusion, such as craving and grasping, which are called "adventitious defilements" in the teachings of Mahamudra. Mind's intrinsic nature, on the other hand, is completely pure and unperturbed.

Unlike non-mental entities or material things in the world, whose nature is empty too, the nature of the mind is not only empty but also luminous *and* cognizant. Emptiness and luminosity co-exist; they exist in a state of unity so should not be seen as two entities. It is only conceptually that we make a distinction between the two. In actual fact, emptiness and luminosity, which are both aspects of the nature of the mind, cannot be separated. That is the basis of purification, the nature of the mind.

The method

The method of purification, in this particular context, is the practice of Mahamudra. According to the Kagyü teachings, for one to take this on board, what is necessary first of all is to find a teacher with the ability to impart the relevant instructions. At the same time, depending upon the teacher and also one's predilections and character traits, one should decide which preliminary practices are necessary before engaging in the actual practice of Mahamudra. For example, in the tantric system generally, it is recommended that practitioners receive certain empowerments or "*abhishekas*," as they are called.

Normally one also engages in the preliminary practice of *ngöndro*, both in its common form, and its uncommon form. The common form involves contemplations that divert the mind away from samsaric concerns, contemplations on such things as the precious human body and the veracity of the law of karma. The uncommon or extraordinary preliminary practice is connected to the practices of prostration, mandala offering, Vajrasattva, and guru yoga. The actual practice of Mahamudra is in the context of the conventional division of meditation practice, namely in its shamatha (tranquility) and vipashyana (insight) forms.

There are four empowerments, or abhishekas, mentioned in the tantric texts: the vase empowerment, the secret empowerment, the empowerment of wisdom, and the word empowerment. These are arranged hierarchically. The vase empowerment, for example, is the most elaborate and ritualistic and deals mainly with the external aspects of religious practice. The later empowerments pertain more to the inner aspects of spiritual experience. With the vase empowerment, for example, a mandala may be constructed of painted sand or something similar, and external objects such as painted figures of deities used to enhance visualization. The later abhishekas or empowerments relate to the inner mandala, where the consciousness, taken as a whole with all its various dimensions and aspects, is seen as the mandala. Generally, these empowerments are taken for specific practices.

At this point it should be mentioned that in most of the traditions of Tibetan Buddhism in general, one is required to follow a graduated path. This incorporates the taking of empowerments and completion of the ordinary and extraordinary practices before embarking on the Mahamudra path. However, according to the Kagyü tradition, this procedure is not always followed rigidly. The manner in which Mahamudra is practiced varies according to certain factors and takes into account the practitioner's level of understanding as well as the skill of the teacher and the time available to them.

It is possible for one to realize Mahamudra even if one has not been able to complete all the preliminary practices. During a moment of contemplation or while remaining in the meditative state, one may come to have direct experience of what is referred to as "ordinary mind," which is another term used for the nature of the mind. Others come to understand, or have realization of Mahamudra, through relying mainly on ritual practices and visualization of deities, using the two stages of the tantric method. The first of these is called the "development stage" and the second, the "fulfillment stage." By relying on these methods and engaging in various yogic exercises, the practitioner may come to have realization of Mahamudra, which is the aim of all tantric practices. In any case, with the specific practice of Mahamudra, through perseverance, the practitioner starts to experience a marked improvement in the stability of the mind during meditation. They also experience a thinning of delusions in their post-meditative experience of the world.

It has to be understood that this way of practicing Mahamudra is unique to the Kagyü tradition. With this approach, one is not leaving Mahamudra practice to the last. Instead, one is practicing Mahamudra along with the other tantric practices, or even before one has received any empowerments at all. Some people have the feeling that going straight to Mahamudra practice without having received the required empowerments or having engaged in other tantric practices is not tantric practice at all. They may simply consider it to be another version of the sutric Mahayana approach where one is able to have a certain realization of emptiness. That, however, is a misunderstanding. All the various practices mentioned in the teachings are used as devices or methods to enhance the development of spiritual understanding. None are fixed and one has to use methods skillfully; one should not be too fixated when it comes to the methods used.

All the various methods used in Tantrism have the one aim, and that is realization of the nature of the mind. If this can be achieved through practice without having received empowerments or engaging in specific tantric practices, then one should do so. In the Kagyü tradition, in fact, it is said that if one has received specific instructions on Mahamudra practice then that constitutes the conferring of a particular type of empowerment. There is such a thing as "transmitting the nature of the mind," and this is considered superior to the empowerments mentioned in standard tantric texts. In any case, the practices associated with Tantrism, such as empowerments, the use of paintings, drawings, rituals, and so on, should be understood properly. They are methods used to give rise to understanding the nature of the mind. If one becomes fixated on them, one has missed the point and the goal has been lost. As a result of this, many Mahamudra masters have said that if one practices the preliminaries and engages in guru yoga, all other tantric methods are included in those practices. This is the method one needs to use in order to overcome the delusions: the practice of Mahamudra.

The object

As mentioned earlier, the nature of the mind has been pure right from the beginning. The object of purification is always pure and immaculate. The adventitious defilements do however exist, and these are what need to be purified. When that has been achieved, another form of purity is accomplished, thus the term "two-fold purity" is used. Although the nature of the mind is pure, due to the adventitious defilements, ordinary human beings do not have the insight to understand the nature of the mind. Once these delusions are removed, two-fold purity has been attained and this is the same as realization of the dharmakaya.

The result

When this two-fold purity has been attained, the practitioner is embodied with two types of wisdom: the wisdom that apprehends the nature of things and of the mind, and the wisdom that apprehends empirical phenomena. Due to realization of these two types of wisdom, one begins to make use of this through wisdom activities, normally referred to as the five types of wisdom—mirror-like wisdom, wisdom of equanimity, wisdom of discrimination, wisdom of accomplishment, and wisdom of dharmakaya.

Verse 8

> *To have cut misconceptions of the ground is the confidence of the view.*
> *To sustain that undistractedly is the key point of meditation.*
> *To train in all the points of practice is the supreme action.*
> *May we possess the confidence of view, meditation and action.*

This verse deals briefly with the view, meditation, and action within Mahamudra practice. In the verses that follow, each of these will be discussed individually.

View

The first line emphasizes the importance of establishing the right view regarding the ground. The word "ground" here refers to the nature of the mind, also known as buddha nature. The way in which the ground is understood within the Mahamudra tradition differs from the Mahayana interpretation of buddha nature. In the sutric or non-tantric teachings of Mahayana Buddhism, buddha nature is normally understood to be a "spark" or a "seed" of enlightenment. While it is considered only a potential and not fully developed, it is also said that because of it, all sentient beings without exception have the capacity to achieve enlightenment at some stage. It is a spark of enlightenment that has remained dormant and is hidden underneath the delusions and obscurations of the mind.

In the context of the Mahamudra teachings, the ground is not spoken about as being simply a spark of enlightenment. It is not considered to be hiding underneath the delusions in a dormant state; it is seen as being fully developed. It is said that the ground or nature of the mind is full and perfect in itself and that nothing needs to be either added to or subtracted from it. Having a grasp of that is what having the correct view means, from the Mahamudra perspective. It is not a question of cultivating buddha nature over a period of time and then attaining enlightenment. Rather, it is a matter of realizing that there is no difference between an enlightened being and an ordinary sentient being, in relation to the ground or the nature of the mind. The difference between an enlightened being and an ordinary sentient being then lies in whether they have knowledge of that fact or are ignorant of it. Sentient beings have not realized that the ground is pure and uncorrupted right from the beginning so they remain in samsara. Buddhas, on the other hand, have come to this recognition.

The ground or nature of the mind needs to be distinguished from normal empirical consciousness, or what is sometimes referred to as "deluded consciousness." This is the consciousness that thinks, that anticipates, that retains memories of all kinds. It also carries the karmic imprints within its continuum. This is the consciousness that is transformed through the practice of meditation. No transformation can take place in relation to the ground or the nature of the mind. For this reason, the verse states, "To have cut misconceptions of the ground is the confidence of the view." To see the ground as being the same as ordinary consciousness or think that the ground is something that can be spoken about in relation to the path and development is a misconception. It is imperative to have a correct grasp of the view regarding the ground.

Meditation

The next line states, "To maintain that undistractedly is the key point of meditation." Having established the right view and having a correct conceptual understanding of the ground then one needs to engage in meditation. This allows one to translate that conceptual understanding into direct experience. According to the approach of Mahamudra meditation, one should not be too concerned with or entangled in ideas of acceptance or rejection. This is unlike the approach of conventional methods of meditation where one tries to cultivate various techniques and antidotes to deal with obstacles that arise during meditation. With the Mahamudra approach, one is not overly concerned with the obstacles that arise in meditation, such as emotional conflicts or delusions. One also does not become too involved with the use of antidotes.

The main point of Mahamudra meditation is to develop stability, on the one hand, and clarity, on the other. Shamatha meditation, as practiced in the Mahamudra tradition, creates the stability, and vipashyana, or insight meditation, gives rise to clarity. With the development of these two qualities, the meditator is able to remain in the state of the ground or the nature of the mind. By simply allowing whatever arises in the mind to rest in its natural state, to rest naturally, one is allowing the thoughts or emotions, whatever they happen to be, to rest in the state of the nature of the mind.

Action

The third line in the verse states, "To train in all the points of practice is the supreme action." As far as action is concerned, one can do all kinds of things to facilitate progress with Mahamudra practice. One may take recourse to certain tantric visualization practices or engage in the practice of the Six Yogas of Naropa,[26] or one can try to maintain a meditative state of mind in post-meditative situations. While there are varieties of things one can do, the most important thing in this context is to have familiarity with the practice of Mahamudra meditation itself. This is the best way of gaining insight into the action aspect.

This verse gives the gist of the Mahamudra outlook, which will be discussed in the following verses. The subsequent verses discuss the right view in more detail and how one comes to it. Then the use of meditation is also described in greater detail, including how the view and meditation are brought to culmination with action, and how the fruition state is obtained.

Verse 9

> *All phenomena are the illusory display of the mind.*
> *Mind is devoid of "mind"—empty of any entity.*
> *Empty and yet unceasing, it manifests as anything whatsoever.*
> *Realizing this completely, may we cut its basis and its root.*

The previous verse in the Mahamudra prayer emphasized the importance of view, meditation, and action, within the context of the Mahamudra tradition. This next verse follows that with a summary of the view. The content of the first line is concerned with how the view is established, according to the Mahamudra approach and tradition. In the approaches taken in the teachings of the sutras, phenomena are examined and analyzed. The right view is arrived at through gaining insight into the nature of everything that exists. With the Mahamudra approach, the mind is emphasized instead. This is possible because insight into reality can be acquired through understanding the nature of the mind itself. In order to do this, first of all one has to realize that everything that exists in the external world is dependent upon the mind because it is the mind that apprehends things through the senses. When one examines one's own experience, one comes to the conclusion that nothing can, in fact, exist independently of the mind. In other words, there is nothing that has objective, self-sufficient, and independent existence.

With the second line, it is pointed out that when this analysis has been carried out and one arrives at the conclusion that nothing can exist independently of the mind, one then has to realize that the mind itself has no independent, inherent existence. Any concept of a pure ego, universal mind, or cosmic consciousness is mistaken, because when the nature of the mind is apprehended it will be revealed as having no definable characteristics; it cannot be empirically determined to be either this or that.

The content of the third line describes how, even though the nature of the mind is understood as lacking in definable characteristics, this does not mean that experiences such as thoughts, ideas, intentions, memory, and expectations come to cease. Experiences continue to arise even when one has gained insight into the nature of the mind-in-itself.

The last line in the verse states that it is important to make use of this analytical procedure so that the ground or the nature of the mind can be properly determined. The verse concludes with: "May one have the ability to do that."

Verse 10

> *We have mistaken our non-existent personal experience*
>   *to be the objects,*
> *And by the power of ignorance, mistaken self-cognizance*
>   *to be a "self."*
> *This dualistic fixation has made us wander in the sphere*
>   *of samsaric existence.*
> *May we cut ignorance and confusion at the very root.*

This verse goes on to elaborate on the view and makes the point that all phenomena are mind-dependent, and this is done in two ways. Firstly, the point is made explicitly, as it is already contained in the verse. There is then also an implicit message, so whilst not articulated in the verse itself, it is nevertheless hinted at. The first line in the verse states that nothing we can call an object can exist of its own accord. In other words, nothing is self-sufficient and independent. The reason this is so is because the *nature* of the mind itself is devoid of characteristics and empirical determinations and therefore empty. Yet, from the point of view of the *essence* of the mind, it is luminous, which is the same as "self-cognizing awareness." The *characteristic* of the mind is what we normally refer to as "the mind" or "consciousness." It is the mind that thinks, intends, remembers, plans, and has various experiences.

Dualistic perception arises as a result of a lack of self-knowledge. In other words, dualistic perception is due to not having a correct understanding of the three aspects of the mind. This refers to understanding the mind in terms of its *nature, essence,* and *characteristic*. Due to this particular erroneous belief, experience becomes divided; one thinks of the mind as the apprehender, and the object of that apprehension as something to be apprehended. One comes to think that what has been apprehended and the apprehender possess independent and self-sufficient existence. This is what ordinary consciousness does. Based upon this mistaken belief, all that is pleasant is seen as something to be sought after and clung onto, and all that is unpleasant is to be rejected and discarded. This experience is what establishes or produces karmic imprints and habitual tendencies. The delusions and emotional conflicts in the mind are then increased. If one is to properly understand how the delusions arise in the mind and how these things come about, one has to know something about how the ego mind operates.

The ego mind has two aspects. The first is to act as reference point for the sensory experiences. This then leaves karmic imprints on the unconscious mind, or what is called *alayavijnana* in Sanskrit, *kunzhi nampar shepa* in Tibetan. The second is to think of the alayavijnana as being the self-existing ego or self. The first aspect of the ego mind is responsible for the experiences of consciousness in normal situations. It is the second aspect of the ego mind that clings onto the alayavijnana as being the locus of self, giving rise to emotional conflicts. The alayavijnana, sometimes called "storehouse-consciousness" or "the unconscious," if you like, acts as the basis for the existence of ego mind. At the same time, it is the alayavijnana that retains the karmic imprints and is responsible for one's habit formation. Therefore there is a causal relationship between the ego mind and the alayavijnana or storehouse-consciousness.

What we normally call "the experience of samsara" is the product of the interaction between the ego mind and the alayavijnana. The ego mind operates due to karmic imprints in the alayavijnana or storehouse-consciousness and with the help of the sensory impressions, sense objects are apprehended as independent of the mind. We see them as having self-sufficient existence, not realizing that these very sense objects are constituted and constructed by the psychic materials arising from the alayavijnana or storehouse-consciousness. In this way, the experience of samsara has to be understood in relation to how the different elements of the mind interact with the sense objects, as well as among themselves and with each other. Even though the nature of the mind itself is free of all empirical determinations and there is no concept of subject and object present in that state, due to ignorance, the essence of the mind that is luminosity or, as it is sometimes called, "self-cognizing awareness," is mistaken for the self.

The basic upshot of this discussion is that the experience of suffering and the errors or diversions that human beings experience on the samsaric level should be attributed to the mind itself. They should not be attributed to anyone or anything else, other than the mind. This is so because suffering is experienced as a result of the misapprehension of reality, and reality has been misapprehended because of the mind. That has occurred because the nature of the mind has not been realized.

So, in fact, this one-to-one correspondence between the deluded experience of the various elements of the mind, and the different aspects of the mind in non-deluded form, is already present within the mind itself. The alayavijnana, or storehouse-consciousness, corresponds to the nature of the mind, which is emptiness. The ego mind corresponds to the luminosity of the mind, or self-cognizing awareness. The ordinary consciousness of the mind corresponds to the characteristic of the mind, where thoughts and concepts arise even in an enlightened state. So it is due to ignorance that these three aspects of the non-deluded mind have not been apprehended and one has gone astray.

The Mahamudra description of how samsara comes into being and exists has a lot to do with the teachings of the third turning of the wheel of the Dharma. What has been said regarding how samsara comes into being and exists is corroborated by these teachings. There are also tantric texts that have put forward similar ideas. According to the tantric teachings, the mind is seen as the key, because it is due to mind that sentient beings are bound to samsara, and also due to mind that they find release. All tantric teachings agree on that point.

The third line of the verse states: "This dualistic fixation has made us wander in the sphere of samsaric existence." The root of the samsaric condition is dualistic fixation, the mind which dichotomizes, which puts things into neat categories—pleasant, unpleasant; good, bad; happiness, unhappiness; bondage and liberation. Until a real revolution on the level of the storehouse-consciousness occurs, there will be no change and there cannot be liberation. The reason for this is that, as has been pointed out, the ego mind depends on the alayavijnana or storehouse-consciousness, and the six sense consciousnesses depend on the ego mind. As long as these different elements of consciousness interact and produce karmic imprints, both positive and negative, then liberation cannot be achieved. The ordinary consciousness that is dominated by dualistic ways of thinking is sustained by the ego mind. The ego mind, in turn, is dependent upon the storehouse-consciousness, so the influence is mutual.

The last line of the verse states: "May we cut ignorance and confusion at the very root." In order to cut at the very root of ignorance, one has to first realize where the error lies. Not only that, one should be able to recognize error for what it is. As long as the error is not recognized there is no way of overcoming it. As Rangjung Dorjé puts it: "May I have the ability to cut at the root of ignorance."

In terms of the content of this verse, as pointed out before, there is also an implicit but not articulated message regarding the mind. We tend to have the feeling that there are things that do have some existence apart from the mind. For instance, we may think that nirvana itself exists apart from the mind because it goes beyond delusion, beyond erroneous beliefs and suffering. It should be made clear that even these things do not have independent existence. If, however, we have been able to understand that all *delusory* experiences are dependent upon the mind then it does not take much effort to understand that everything that is *non-delusory* is also dependent upon the mind.

The mind in its deluded form is referred to as "mind," "consciousness," "ego mind," or "ego consciousness," but even in its non-deluded form things still have to be understood in terms of the mind. It is still the mind that is being talked about, whether it is in deluded form or non-deluded form, and enlightenment is spoken about in relation to how much delusion is present in the mind. This has been made very clear in teachings like the *Highest Continuum*[27]. Sometimes teachers such as Chandrakirti have made the point that when the fire of insight consumes the karmic imprints, the mind comes to cease to exist and one realizes the changeless nature of dharmakaya. When it is said that the mind comes to "cease," though, this does not mean that at the time of enlightenment the mind *actually* comes to cease. It means that the mind has become transformed on a manifest level. At the same time, one has realized the nature of the mind as-it-is. As far as the nature of the mind itself is concerned, it is the dharmakaya; it does not exist in time and space. The wisdom of the buddha is based upon the same mind that sentient beings possess. The mind of the buddha cannot be found elsewhere.

Enlightenment is a relative concept; when there is less delusion there is more enlightenment. It is, nevertheless, the same mind. In this way, the verse establishes the importance of realizing how everything depends upon the mind. This has been pointed out in two ways, explicitly and implicitly—explicitly, in terms of how delusions come into being and implicitly, in relation to how even the things that are sublime and transcendent are ultimately dependent upon the mind. For this reason, tantric texts such as

Wheel of Time[28] have stated, "When the mind is not understood one dwells in samsara; when the mind is understood one becomes enlightened but, apart from the mind, there is no buddhahood."

This verse emphasized the importance of seeing how everything is dependent upon the mind, understanding that nothing that is knowable can exist apart from the mind itself. The next two verses are concerned with discussion of the mind itself.

Verse 11

It is not existent since even the victorious ones do not see it.
It is not non-existent since it is the basis of samsara and nirvana.
This is not a contradiction, but the Middle Way of unity.
May we realize the nature of mind, free from extremes.

The first line in the verse discusses the unconditioned or absolute aspect of the mind, namely, the nature of the mind. The second line discusses the relative mind or empirical consciousness and its relationship to the nature of the mind.

In the previous verse, it was said that everything that can be experienced, both within and without, is dependent upon the mind. But when one examines the nature of the mind—the unconditioned aspect that ordinary sentient beings are not aware of—it reveals itself as lacking empirical characteristics and determination. It cannot, therefore, be identified as being this or that. The nature of the mind cannot be discovered as dwelling in a particular place, such as within or without, for the simple reason that it is unconditioned and not causally produced. The absolute aspect of the mind is something that cannot be represented in any way or even conceptually formulated. That is why, in the sutras, it has been said that the nature of the mind is something that even the enlightened ones, the buddhas, have not perceived. Such statements are made because "to perceive" means that something or other is perceived as having such-and-such definable characteristics and can be described and formulated with concepts and words. This is not possible with something that is unconditioned, as is the absolute aspect of the mind.

As mentioned earlier, the nature of the mind, the absolute or unconditioned aspect of the mind, should be distinguished from the normal or ordinary consciousness that sentient beings are immediately aware of. The mind that is responsible for having sensations or feelings, the mind which can produce conceptual constructs and create mental propensities, the mind that gives rise to thought of a self, an apprehender or perceiver, is the ordinary or relative aspect of the mind. These two aspects of the mind have to be distinguished. One is unconditioned and the other is conditioned; the first is absolute, the second relative. The unconditioned aspect of the mind is distinguished from thoughts, perceptions, and conceptions. It is not something that can be perceived or identified or represented in any way, so even the enlightened beings have not seen it. Whenever meditators come across statements that imply that there is something called "nature of the mind" which can be perceived, then they have to understand that statement metaphorically and not literally. Even when it is said that meditators will be able to perceive the nature of the mind, that does not mean that they will perceive the nature of the mind in a literal sense.

The same thing can be said about the aspect of luminosity, also known as "self-cognizing awareness" or "self-cognizing wisdom." When the term "self-cognition" is used, again, that has to be understood metaphorically rather than seeing it as the mind intending upon itself, using an aspect of itself as the object of its intent or awareness. In certain Mahayana sutra teachings, one even finds the idea of self-cognizing consciousness criticized. So, when it is said that the nature of the mind has the aspect of luminosity then one should think of that in terms of the analogy of a lamp. A lamp does not illuminate itself; a lamp illuminates everything else. It dispels darkness in the surrounding area but does not illuminate itself because there is no darkness within its flame.

Returning to the verse, the first line describes the importance of distinguishing the absolute and unconditioned aspect of the mind from the conditioned aspect, and the second describes the conditioned aspect of the mind. From the point of view of the absolute aspect of the mind, the mind has no definable characteristics. It is the same as emptiness. However, from the point of view of the relative aspect of the mind then it does have certain definable characteristics; there are mental activities. This is normally described as "the play of the mind" in Mahamudra literature. But what has to be realized is that the existence of the relative aspect of the mind is made possible because of its unconditioned aspect. Without the unconditioned aspect of the mind, concepts of samsara or bondage, and nirvana or freedom would have no relevance. This is so because ideas of spiritual bondage and freedom are defined in relation to the presence or absence of this recognition of the unconditioned aspect of the mind. If an individual has recognized the unconditioned aspect of the mind, which ordinary beings are not aware of or in tune with, then such a person is described as an enlightened being. Failure to achieve this causes one to wander continuously in samsaric existence. The unconditioned aspect of the mind is responsible for one's experiences, in terms of the experiences one endures on the level of samsaric existence, those involved with being on the path, and also those on the level of enlightenment.

In this way, the meditator of the Mahamudra tradition can avoid the two extremes of eternalism and nihilism. The pitfall of eternalism is avoided by development of a correct concept of the unconditioned aspect of the mind: not thinking of it as some kind of unchanging substance, but realizing that the unconditioned or absolute aspect of the mind is free of empirical determinations and is a state of total openness creating room for everything to arise. The other pitfall, which is nihilism, is avoided by the concept of the relative or conditioned aspect of the mind. Even though the absolute aspect of the mind, the nature of the mind, is devoid of characteristics, nevertheless, the conditioned aspect of the mind does not cease to operate. Thoughts, concepts, feelings, and emotions continue to arise.

To develop the view of the mind as a whole is to have a clear understanding of these two aspects. This clear understanding in no way emphasizes one aspect at the expense of the other and the meditator realizes how these two aspects co-exist in a harmonious fashion. If one fails to do this, by emphasizing the unconditioned aspect of the nature of the mind, for example, and neglecting the relative or conditioned aspect of the mind, then that would lead to an erroneous view. As Nagarjuna puts it, "Those individuals who hold onto the unconditioned, which is the same as emptiness, as being real in itself, can only cause more harm; it will have no liberating effect and they will fall into the extreme of nihilism."

The third line in the verse points out that there is no contradiction between what has been said in the first and second lines, because the mind does not exist in a substantial sense, due to its unconditioned aspect. At the same time, it is not non-existent because unceasing mental activities arise from its relative aspect. So when one looks into it properly, there is no contradiction. It is not saying that one thing exists and does not exist at the same time, which would be a logical contradiction. This is the middle view in relation to the Mahamudra tradition. However, this way of describing the middle view is slightly different from the sutric teachings of Madhyamaka insofar as the middle view has been established in relation to the mind, rather than in relation to emptiness. In any case, the middle view of Mahamudra is maintained by not over-exaggerating one aspect of the mind and underestimating the other. In order to have proper understanding of the mind, one has to understand these two aspects and how they co-exist in a harmonious way without conflict. One aspect is no more important than the other. One has to have this total appreciation of how the mind works.

Verse 12

> *Nothing can illustrate it by the statement, "This is it."*
> *No one can deny it by saying, "This is not it."*
> *This nature transcending concepts is unconditioned.*
> *May we realize this view of the true meaning.*

The content of this verse does not differ greatly from the previous one. The difference lies in the fact that this verse concentrates exclusively on the nature of the mind, whereas in the previous verse the idea of avoiding the two kinds of extremes was emphasized.

According to the first line, "Nothing can illustrate it by the statement 'this is it.'" This line makes the point that the nature of the mind is not something that can be described in a positive way— not "positive" in terms of moral or aesthetic values, but "positive" in the sense of conceptuality. From the ultimate point of view, the nature of mind cannot be described as having this or that attribute. In the teachings, the nature of mind may be described as the same as "emptiness," "unoriginatedness," "the absolute," "co-emergent wisdom," and "great bliss." All these words are used to refer to the nature of the mind, but the nature of the mind cannot be represented by any of these words.

These words should be understood as metaphors describing the nature of the mind rather than as words genuinely referring to the nature of the mind as such. The reason for this is that the nature of the mind is unconditioned and lacks any of the discoverable features of an entity; it cannot be represented as being this or that. It is important to remember that even when words such as "emptiness," "unoriginatedness," "the absolute," "co-emergent wisdom," and "great bliss" are used, they are always used in a metaphorical way. We should not think that there is some corresponding relationship to be obtained between the words and the referent, which is the nature of the mind. Furthermore, from the ultimate point of view, the nature of the mind cannot be said to be either plural or unitary, eternal or temporal. In brief, the nature of the mind does not display any of the characteristics of conditioned phenomena.

The second line states, "No one can deny it by saying 'it is not this.'" Now, despite the fact that the nature of the mind does not have the relevant characteristics, attributes, or properties of an entity, it cannot be denied; its existence cannot be negated. The reason the existence of the nature of the mind cannot be negated is because it has never come into being. Only conditioned things, things which possess properties, qualities, characteristics, or attributes can be proven to exist or not exist through the use of logic. Because the nature of the mind does not possess such properties in the first place, its existence cannot be denied either. When the first line of the verse says that the nature of the mind cannot be represented by this or that, not having characteristics of such and such a nature, it does not mean that the nature of the mind does not exist. For these two reasons the nature of the mind is indescribable, going beyond conceptual constructs.

As the line, "This nature transcending concepts is unconditioned" points out, that which is unconditioned can be described in this particular way. Only unconditioned phenomena can go beyond empirical determinations, precisely because they cannot be described as existing in the way that ordinary things or mental events exist—that is, as having properties. Nor can unconditioned phenomena be denied existence altogether because, even though the nature of the mind lacks the usual characteristics and properties of empirical phenomena, it still cannot be described as being nonexistent. To understand this, one must go beyond conceptual constructs and have an immediate experience of the nature of the mind. These unconditioned phenomena, *asamskrita* in Sanskrit, *dumajé* in Tibetan, mean that everything that we experience through the senses and all conditioned phenomena are the product of causes and conditions. The nature of the mind, however, is unconditioned. Everything that is conditioned has come into being through varieties of factors but that which is unconditioned is unproduced, unchanging, eternal, empty of inherent existence and devoid of characteristics, qualities, or attributes.

The last line in the verse reads, "May we realize this view of the true meaning." Rangjung Dorjé, the author of the song, wishes that the practitioner may come to have correct understanding of the nature of the mind through the practice of meditation, an understanding which is not assailed by doubts and uncertainties but based instead upon certainty and confidence.

These teachings about the nature of the mind make it very clear that our everyday experience of the mind is not to be undervalued or thought to be unimportant. It is, in fact, very important. Where the real illusion lies is in thinking that everyday experience is what reality is, thinking that the experience of consciousness that we have in normal circumstances and situations is the only reality there is and that there is nothing more to it. It is very important to have the correct understanding of the mind. We begin to realize that the mind has two aspects, the conditioned aspect and the unconditioned aspect, and that people normally have access to and understanding of the conditioned aspect of the mind, but not the unconditioned aspect.

Through practices such as Mahamudra meditation we can develop a total understanding of the mind. However, if we deny the conditioned aspect of the mind then we have to deny the reality of the path. The spiritual path or the idea of purification of the mind or spiritual development involves dealing with the mind that has certain characteristics, attributes, and properties. I think it's very important to have that understanding and thus avoid falling into either of those two extremes. The point of the previous verse was to bring out the importance of not falling into either of those extremes—the extreme of ignoring ordinary conscious experience or the extreme of being completely immersed in the everyday experience of the world and the inner workings of consciousness.

Verse 13

Without realizing this, we circle through the ocean of samsara.
When realizing it, buddhahood is not somewhere else.
It is completely devoid of "it is this" or "it is not this."
May we see this vital point of the all-ground, the nature of things.

The reason ordinary sentient beings continue to suffer and wander about in the samsaric condition is because they have not understood the nature of the mind. If the nature of the mind is realized then that is the same as attaining buddhahood. There are two kinds of movement taking place when an ordinary sentient being attains enlightenment or realizes the nature of the mind. One movement goes backward in the sense that the nature of the mind, which is not different from the essential nature of sentient beings, has been retrieved. Realizing the nature of the mind is not something new; it is a retrieval of one's essential nature. This essential nature had remained obscured or concealed because of delusions and ignorance. At the same time, there is a movement that takes place which is forward-directed. It is forward-directed insofar as when the nature of the mind is realized then one becomes much more than one has been in the past, though one does so while remaining in the world as an ordinary sentient being. To realize buddhahood or enlightenment is to actualize one's essential nature, which has always been there yet, at the same time, it is to become much more than one has been in the past. An ordinary sentient being becomes an enlightened being.

This idea of retrieval is somewhat unique to the Mahamudra teachings but is also to be found in certain Mahayana literature belonging to the school of Yogacara[29] philosophy. For example, the idea of attaining enlightenment can be spoken of only in relation to the relative aspect of the mind. From the point of view of the nature of the mind, which is unchanging and ever-present, one cannot describe it in any way as being this or that. As the verse says, "It is completely devoid of 'it is this' or 'it is not this.'" One becomes enlightened through understanding the relationship between the relative and absolute aspects of the mind.

The verse concludes with the wish that we, as practitioners, have the ability to realize the vital point of the "all-ground." This "all-ground" is a synonym for the nature of the mind, because both ignorance and wisdom arise from the alaya. The alaya should be distinguished from alayavijnana, or storehouse-consciousness. This was discussed earlier in the prayer, where alayavijnana was seen as the ground from which all the samsaric experiences arise.

Verse 14

> *Perceiving is mind, being empty is also mind.*
> *Realizing is mind, being mistaken is also mind.*
> *Having arisen is mind, having ceased is also mind.*
> *May we cut through all our doubts concerning mind.*

As has already been pointed out, enlightenment cannot be

achieved unless one has a correct understanding of the mind. Everything is dependent upon the mind. If we think in terms of our empirical experience of the world—our sense experiences, our emotions and thoughts, in other words all the experiences that occur within the mind and all the experiences of the world apprehended through the senses—all of these are dependent upon the mind. Nothing can exist independently of the mind precisely because nothing can be apprehended without the use of the mind and its abilities. As stated in the first line of the verse, "perceiving is mind"— meaning appearances are mind—and then the line goes on, "being empty is also mind." When we talk about the nature of reality or the nature of things, not only in terms of how things appear to the mind, but also how things exist and their nature, which is emptiness—even then we cannot talk about it apart from the mind. This is because emptiness is apprehended and experienced through the mind and the nature of the mind is no different from emptiness.

The second line reads, "Realizing is mind, being mistaken is also mind." "Realizing is mind" refers to the meditator or practitioner realizing the mind through cultivation of greater awareness and gaining further insight into the workings of the mind, in terms of both its relative and absolute aspects. "Being mistaken is also mind" means that when one remains in the samsaric condition and perceives everything from a dualistic point of view, thinking that there is an immutable unchanging self as the perceiver and an objective world which exists of its own accord as an object of perception, these kinds of erroneous beliefs and experiences are also a product of the mind.

The understanding of the nature of the mind is obtained through gaining an appreciation of how ground, path, and fruition Mahamudra are related to each other. Ground Mahamudra is the nature of the mind itself. Even when sentient beings are oblivious of its existence or presence, still, it is there. Path Mahamudra has to do with the practice of Mahamudra, which leads to the realization of fruition Mahamudra, which is none other than ground Mahamudra. These three different aspects of Mahamudra have to be understood in relation to the mind.

The samsaric experiences of sentient beings, generated by the mistaken belief in the duality of subject and object, are also a product of the mind. In the third line, Rangjung Dorjé makes the statement, "Having arisen is mind, having ceased is also mind." What this means is that the delusions that have arisen in the mind are also a product of the mind and the way in which these delusions come to cease to exist is also brought about by the mind. Rangjung Dorjé concludes the verse by saying, "May we cut through all our doubts concerning mind." This is a prayer that we have the ability to cut through doubts in order to realize that the mind is the most powerful thing. There is nothing other than the mind that can lead us out. The mind is responsible for the samsaric condition and the suffering that it induces, and also for the liberation and enlightenment that comes from understanding the nature of the mind.

That concludes the explanation of the nature of the mind and its relationship to ordinary consciousness or the relative aspect of the mind. Beginning with the next verse, the prayer explains the Mahamudra practices that lead the practitioner to realize Mahamudra or the nature of the mind.

Verse 15

Unspoiled by intellectual and deliberate meditation,
And unmoved by the winds of ordinary distractions,
May we be skilled in sustaining the practice of mind
  essence,
Being able to rest in unfabricated and innate naturalness.

So far we have discussed the importance of realizing the nature of the mind and of understanding how the empirical, relative aspect relates to the nature of the mind. We have also looked at how one's perception of the phenomenal world is essentially dependent upon the constitution of the mind. We will now come to discuss the methods used to understand the nature of the mind.

There is only one method, which is meditation. Meditation is best explained by commenting on the second line of the verse which states, "And unmoved by the winds of ordinary distractions." It is essential as a practitioner to have some skill in observing one's experiences, speech, and behavior. The fundamental cause of flaws in the human condition comes from not exercising sufficient awareness in relation to the three gates, namely body, speech, and mind. It is therefore necessary to create an environment where one is not so easily provoked or stimulated, where one can drop all the ordinary concerns of happiness and unhappiness, gain and loss, and so forth. If this sort of environment is not created for meditation, then not only is one unable to achieve enlightenment, but even the possibility of securing liberation is curtailed. This is why the second line in the verse begins, "And unmoved by the winds of ordinary distractions." When an appropriate environment is created for meditation, it is easier for the meditator to have a relaxed state of mind and keep distraction at bay.

There is a story told by an Indian mahasiddha known as Avadhut,[30] regarding how distractions can be avoided. He uses different examples, allegorical in nature, to describe how he understands the significance of gaining a stabilized mind, a focused mind. Firstly, Avadhut realizes that being hopeful is not conducive to securing a concentrated and focused mind. He observes a woman who falls in love with a man and develops a deep friendship with him. One day the man leaves, saying to the woman, "I will return." The woman is hopeful that he will, in fact, turn up—if not that day then perhaps the day after, and if not the day after, then perhaps the next week, and so on. Through this, Avadhut realizes that being hopeful, even in terms of wanting to become enlightened, is not beneficial.

Avadhut also notices that being competitive distracts the mind. When a group of seagulls gathers and one of them picks up some food, all the others want to take the food away from it, and a struggle ensues. Therefore, when it comes to the practice of meditation, one should not have a competitive mind, for example, wanting to meditate for longer than the next person so you can prove that you can sit longer.

In a similar way, Avadhut says that a meditator should not feel overly comfortable with wherever they are, but rather develop a sense of homelessness, a sense of not feeling too secure. He observes a female snake lying comfortably in its nest. She lays eggs which turn into little snakes and the nest becomes crowded, but rather than remaining in the nest with her young and feeling too comfortable, she decides to make another nest. Avadhut says it is very important not to feel too comfortable wherever one is at any given moment. The meditator should have a feeling of homelessness, of being able to make a transition or change, just like the mother snake.

Avadhut also points out that a meditator should be self-reliant rather than being too dependent upon other people's opinions and expectations. This is brought home by what he observes with respect to a hunter in the wilderness. The hunter has no companions, lives alone, and does not need companionship. In a similar way, the meditator should be self-reliant; having a sense of basic self-trust.

Finally, Avadhut realizes the importance of a focused mind. He does this when he sees how an arrow-maker fashions an arrow with complete concentration. The meditator, too, must embody such a concentrated mind. With these examples, he makes it clear that abandonment of mental distractions is the starting point for meditation.

The third line adds, "May we be skilled in sustaining the practice of mind essence." Having created the environment, as discussed, and having achieved a certain level of assurance in the stability of the mind, the meditator should concentrate on how to settle the mind in its natural state. This is brought about by allowing the effusive thought-flows of the mind to rest in their own natural state; in other words, by not contriving the mind, not trying to do something unnatural or condition the mind.

Prior to attempting this, it is important to concentrate on the posture of the body, because if correct posture is not maintained it is difficult to let the mind rest in its natural state. The fundamental posture of meditation consists of sitting on a comfortable cushion that is not too hard, not too soft, not too high, and not too low. One's gaze should be directed downwards so that one is aware of the tip of the nose. The shoulders should be even; one shoulder not being higher than the other. One should not clench one's teeth; they should be open in a comfortable position, and the breath even. This position is regarded as the most efficient way to develop the meditative state of mind.

While holding this position, one should try to allow one's mind to remain in its own natural state. This is the meaning of the first line of the verse, "Unspoiled by intellectual and deliberate meditation." After having sat down on the cushion, the practitioner of Mahamudra should no longer be concerned about such things as what a meditative state of mind is, what the nature of the mind is, or the relationship between the nature of mind, which is the absolute aspect of mind, and the relative aspect. The meditator should not think of any of these things. In fact, it is said in relation to Mahamudra that shamatha or meditation of tranquility requires that all thoughts of the meditator, the meditation, and the object of meditation should be put to rest. This is the only way the meditator can allow the mind to rest in its own natural state. When thoughts and emotions arise, they should be noticed, but then let go. One should not judge them as being positive or negative; beneficial or harmful.

For this reason, it is said that when the practitioner of Mahamudra engages in shamatha, meditation of tranquility, they should do so with a sense of ease. The element of ease is there when the meditator is not concerned about either creating a tranquil state of mind or preventing certain unpleasant states of mind from arising. Whatever arises in the mind, be it pleasant or unpleasant, beneficial or harmful, beautiful or repulsive, should be viewed as the play of the mind. Just as people in an audience watching a play do not take everything that goes on in the play to be real and become completely overwhelmed, so the meditator in a similar way should view whatever goes on in the mind. One should observe and take notice of whatever goes on but not be swayed by it. When the meditator is able to adopt such an attitude, the mind naturally rests in its natural state. It is only a habit of the mind to constantly react to things in this or that way. This obviously, naturally leads to distraction of the mind. A practitioner of Mahamudra should not think the aim is to create a positive state of mind and prevent negative states of mind from arising but should let the mind be in its natural state while being observant of whatever is occurring in the mind.

This state of meditation has two aspects. The first is not to condition the mind, but to allow it to be without contrivance. The second aspect is the natural condition of the mind. These two correlate. When the mind is not conditioned, it rests in its own natural state. The way to achieve this is not to follow one's mind in relation to memories and past experiences and not to anticipate future experiences. One does not dwell on either happy memories or painful memories, the memories of the past, nor does one anticipate the future, thinking of it in terms of fear or anxiety or looking forward to it with a sense of hopefulness. In terms of present mental occurrences, one should simply take notice of them without thinking such things as: "this is pleasant," "this is comforting," "this is painful," "this is disturbing.. This is one of the main pieces of advice given to us by Gampopa, one of the forefathers of the Kagyü lineage and the foremost student of Milarepa. The gist of this Mahamudra meditation technique is—as the Tibetan saying goes—"When the mind is left undisturbed it is clear, and when a pond is not stirred it is not muddy." In this way, as the first line of this verse describes it, "Unspoiled by intellectual and deliberate meditation," the mind should be left in its own natural state.

According to the Mahamudra approach to meditation, one should not be concerned with past experiences or be anticipating future events but, rather, one should try to remain in a state of naturalness, which does not mean one should be fixated on the present experience either. As Saraha points out in his doha songs, "When the meditator has abandoned thoughts concerning the three times, namely the past, present, and future, and is able to remain in the natural state of mind, such a state is considered to be a formal meditation."

The fundamental point regarding the Mahamudra approach to meditation is the element of effortlessness. This means that the meditator does not apply exertion with any thought of securing the meditative state, but it is about letting the mind rest in its own natural state. Letting the mind "be" is realizing the nature of the mind itself. In other words, the nature of the mind is realized when the mind is left in its own original, natural, uncontrived state. When the meditator is able to remain in such a state though, again, it is necessary to ensure that there is no clinging to that experience.

Some have criticized the system of Mahamudra, alleging that it encourages a state of total thoughtlessness. In fact, certain Tibetan Buddhist scholars have said that the type of meditative experience encouraged by the Mahamudra tradition is comparable to the early Ch'an or Zen tradition of China introduced to the Tibetans very early on in the history of Tibetan Buddhism. This is a misunderstanding on the part of critics for the simple reason that the Mahamudra approach to meditation does not encourage the meditator to empty their mind of all its contents by applying an element of force or effort, through deliberation. On the contrary, no matter what the content of the mind is at any given moment, that very mental state is used to achieve self-liberation. This is accomplished through letting the thought or emotion or whatever happens to be present in the mind, be there without clinging and without elaboration. "Not to be concerned with the three times" does not mean that one has to make a deliberate effort not to be concerned with the past, present, or future. Rather, one should allow the mind to be in its own natural state, in the present. When the mind is let loose in this manner, thoughts related to the three times naturally subside; no effort is necessary. Therefore, the essence of Mahamudra meditation is not to empty the mind of all its contents through the force of employing certain techniques but, rather, to let it be in its own natural condition.

This type of meditation is considered superior to many other methods of meditation within the Buddhist tradition. This is so because the Mahamudra approach is non-symbolic, non-referential and so it is superior to other types that are symbolic and referential in orientation. This point has been made very clearly in such tantric literature as the *Wheel of Time*. Here, it is said that while the meditator may have to use certain images, such as deities, seed syllables, or certain spiritual items like vajra, lotus, and so on, these things are only used in order to realize that which, by its own nature, is non-representational and cannot be symbolized. It is possible to rely on certain tantric methods and in this way one may be able to realize the nature of the mind which cannot be symbolized, and which is non-referential. However, if one relies on the practice of Mahamudra meditation, based on the idea of immediately entering into the natural state of the mind then, once that is realized, everything that could be attained or realized through tantric methods is already embodied in this approach.

As a Mahamudra practitioner, as soon as one has been able to ease oneself onto the cushion, one should divest one's mind of all thoughts concerning such things as the meditation, the meditator, and the object of meditation. In such a state of mind, one does not need to think about deities, mantras, or anything of the sort; one simply remains in that natural state of openness. As long as the meditator is caught up with thoughts of meditation, the meditator, or the object of meditation, they cannot remain in the natural state of the mind. The key point in the practice of Mahamudra meditation is unwavering awareness. "Unwavering awareness" means paying attention to whatever has arisen in the mind with the understanding that it is causally produced; that every thought, every emotion that has arisen in the mind is connected to certain causes and conditions. Paying attention to them, being aware of them and letting them be, leads the meditator to the realization of the nature of the mind, which is not causally produced and is unconditioned.

Being able to do that is the same as realizing Mahamudra; Mahamudra is no other than this. A person who is pursuing the practice of Mahamudra meditation should not be concerned about whether they are meditating properly, whether they are overwhelmed by this or that thought or whether they are becoming anxious about wanting to get better at the practice of meditation. Having made oneself comfortable on the meditation cushion, one should not entertain such thoughts but try to remain in a state of naturalness by being aware of whatever arises in the mind at any given moment.

Even though this is the Mahamudra approach and superior to all the other practices used in the tantric tradition, it may, in fact, be helpful for most people to engage in some tantric practices that deal with symbols, such as the visualization of deities and seed syllables, and use meditation in conjunction with tantric yogic exercises, and so on. Even then, the meditator should always keep in mind that these methods are stepping stones to the realization of Mahamudrahood. The idea is that, with the skillful use of symbolic and representational methods, one will realize that which cannot be symbolized, that which is non-representational. This is the meaning of the last line of the verse, "Being able to rest in unfabricated and innate naturalness."

Verse 16

> *The waves of gross and subtle thoughts having*
>   *spontaneously subsided,*
> *The river of unwavering mind naturally abides.*
> *Free from the stains of dullness, sluggishness and*
>   *conceptualization,*
> *May we be stable in the unmoving ocean of shamatha.*

As has already been mentioned, the object of Mahamudra meditation is to go beyond anything representational, symbolic, and conceptual. In order to arrive at that state, however, first of all, one has to engage in the practice of settling the mind. This can be achieved only through the practice of shamatha, meditation of tranquility. "Settling the mind" basically means that one attempts to focus one's mind on the object of meditation, thereby neutralizing the disturbances of emotional conflicts and discursive thoughts. When the mind is focused and the level of concentration maintained, disturbances in the mind no longer have any effect on its stability. All disturbances in the mind arise from these two sources, emotional conflict and discursive thought. These arise only when the mind is distracted. They do not have the same effect on a concentrated mind as they do on a distracted mind.

The first line in the verse reads, "The waves of gross and subtle thoughts having spontaneously subsided…" Shamatha meditation has to be cultivated in order to deal with the gross level of disturbances, which are both emotional and conceptual in content and which arise when the meditator is conscious of them. The subtle disturbances are those mental activities, thoughts, and emotions that the meditator may endure at any given moment but be unable to detect and which one may remain unconscious or unaware of.

These various mental disturbances arising in the mind are compared to the ebb and flow of waves: "The waves of gross and subtle thoughts having spontaneously subsided…" The waves of thoughts and emotions are not actively stopped by the meditator. The disturbances are not prevented from arising through the deliberate use of technique but, rather, through a process of recognition they naturally come to subside, in the same way as the waves on the surface of the ocean naturally blend into the ocean when they crash back into the sea. In a similar way, these disturbances arise in the mind and then they dissipate back into the natural state of the mind without deliberate effort to remove them. If that is done, then, as the second line in the verse reads, "The river of unwavering mind naturally abides." If one does not consciously try to stop thinking, or consciously try to prevent anger, desire, lust, or jealousy from arising in the mind, then one will be able to remain in the natural state of the mind. The mind naturally comes to rest in that position.

The third line of the verse is, "Free from the stains of dullness, sluggishness and conceptualization…" Fundamentally, there are only two obstacles the meditator should attend to or be aware of: dullness or sluggishness, and agitation. If we want to elaborate on this, we can talk about five obstacles. These five obstacles, however, are basically variations of the two primary ones. As *Letter to a Friend*,[31] a text written by the great Mahayana master Nagarjuna, states, "There are five obstacles to meditation. The first is extreme agitation of the mind, the second is regret or guilt, the third is ill will, the fourth is sluggishness and the fifth is doubt." Another way to understand this is to combine extreme agitation of the mind and guilt together, and then group ill will, sloth, and obsession, with sensual indulgence and doubt. These obstacles have to be understood in relation to the practice of meditation itself. If the mind is out-flowing and follows the senses then it becomes agitated. Guilt or regret comes from recognizing that the mind has become distracted. Upon this recognition, the meditator may become bogged down by guilt. This occurs as a result of not having been able to maintain mindfulness and awareness. Agitation and regret prevent the meditator from maintaining a peaceful mind.

Ill will is a hindrance insofar as while it persists, the meditator is not able to maintain a sense of joyfulness. Sloth causes the meditator to lose clarity of mind, with the result that the mind becomes dim and opaque. Sloth is therefore an obstacle to the maintenance of clarity, which is essential to achieving a meditative state. Obsessive thoughts of sensual indulgence, in terms of either animate or inanimate objects, can be an obstacle to the workability of the mind, its flexibility or pliancy. Finally, entertaining doubts about whether one is meditating properly, whether one is in a meditative state, or whether one's experience is real or imagined, disrupts the one-pointed concentration of meditation. However, as pointed out earlier, these five obstacles are basically variations of the two primary obstacles, as can be gleaned from the list given—the two primary obstacles being sluggishness and mental agitation.

The method used to overcome these obstacles in the context of Mahamudra differs from that of the other traditions in that all that is required is to recognize, identify, and become aware of them. Nothing more is necessary. There is no need to apply antidotes to overcome these obstacles. Having recognized and identified them, one should allow them to rest in their natural state. By doing so, the meditator is able to establish the right foundation for attainment of shamatha, meditation of tranquility. As Shantideva,[32] another great Mahayana master, has said, "Once the emotional conflicts have been brought under control through the practice of shamatha then the meditator should proceed to the practice of vipashyana or insight meditation." It is essential that meditators develop shamatha as the foundation for their practice. Without a focused mind it is very difficult to advance spiritually, even though one may be engaged in varieties of practices and may employ various techniques to induce spiritual realization or enlightenment.

Rangjung Dorjé concludes the verse by saying, "May we be stable in the unmoving ocean of shamatha." This refers to the notion that disturbances in the mind subside naturally through the use of the technique of Mahamudra, which is simply to recognize and identify them. Just like the waves that arise from the ocean naturally fall back into the ocean, in a similar way, "May the meditator's experience of agitation, brought on by emotional conflicts and discursive thoughts, subside back into the ocean of the nature of the mind and the ocean-like shamatha be achieved."

Verse 17

When looking again and again into the unseen mind,
The fact that there is nothing to see is vividly seen as it is.
Cutting through doubts about its nature being existent or
  nonexistent,
May we unmistakenly recognize our own essence.

When the meditator comes to a particular point with their practice of shamatha, as described and set forth in the previous verse, they realize the importance of vipashyana or insight meditation. Insight is attained by looking into the nature of the mind. The practice of shamatha or meditation of tranquility deals only with the conditioned aspect of the mind. This is to say that the meditator attempts to deal with conflicting emotions and conceptual proliferations as they arise during meditation, by applying mindfulness and awareness. With vipashyana or insight meditation, the meditator has to go beyond that. As a result, the meditator attains certain intimation of the nature of the mind itself, which is the unconditioned aspect of the mind.

When the word "insight" is used in this context, it has to be understood in a non-relational sense, because there is no difference between insight and the object of insight. This is so for the simple reason that the nature of the mind does not present itself as being this or that, like normal mental states or events such as thoughts and emotions. For this reason, the second line in the verse says "there is nothing to see," which means that the nature of the mind does not present itself as an entity of any kind. It cannot be comprehended with our normal concepts of substance and attributes, subject and predicate, and so on. A part of vipashyana, or insight meditation practice, involves looking deeper and deeper into the mind so that what cannot be seen is seen, precisely and properly. The line in the verse reads, "The fact that there is nothing to see is vividly seen as it is." "Insight," in this case, does not mean insight into any particular aspect or state of the mind, but rather insight into the mind as a whole.

In order to perceive the nature of the mind, the unconditioned aspect of the mind, one even has to abandon the whole notion of existence or nonexistence of the mind. This is expressed in the third line, "Cutting through doubts about its nature being existent or nonexistent..." These concepts are applicable only to the conditioned aspect of the mind or empirical consciousness, the aspect which feels, thinks, anticipates, plans, and so forth. They are not applicable to the non-conditioned aspect of the mind. Even the uncertainty that one may feel regarding the nature of the mind, where one may have such thoughts as "Does it exist?" or "Does it not exist?" is completely irrelevant in relation to the nature of the mind.

The last line of the verse reads, "May we unmistakenly recognize our own essence." Here, it needs to be pointed out that this line can be understood in two different ways. First, we can understand it as saying, "May the meditator have the ability to have an undiluted experience of the nature of the mind, which is one's own nature." The other way to understand this is that the nature of the mind itself is free from distortion, free from defilements. To recognize that the nature of the mind is intrinsically immaculate from its own side is to recognize one's own nature. It's like recognizing one's own true face. To recognize the nature of the mind is the equivalent of recognizing one's own true nature, which has never been corrupted by the goings-on at the empirical level of consciousness. This recognition is no different from the realization of Mahamudrahood.

Verse 18

When observing objects, they are seen to be the mind, devoid of objects.
When observing the mind, there is no mind, as it is empty of an entity.
When observing both, dualistic fixation is spontaneously freed.
May we realize the natural state of the luminous mind.

The *Aspiration of Mahamudra* further elucidates the view of emptiness with the above verse. The first line of the verse, "When observing objects, they are seen to be the mind, devoid of objects," means that an individual observes the world through the senses. The only way the external, material world can be apprehended is through visual and auditory sensations, and so forth. However, by focusing on these sensory impressions, one concludes that anything one may understand about the external world is dependent upon the mind. Any information one receives about the world through the senses is already vitiated by conceptual constructs. One perceives individual things in the world as being this or that, as being chairs or tables or a mountain, and so forth. Through this, the meditator realizes there is no external material world existing of its own accord, independent of the mind. In this way, the meditator comes to understand that the mind is not passive; it is not a receptacle. Rather, the mind is both active and creative. How the world is apprehended through an individual's senses is determined by the conceptual schema of the mind itself.

The second line of the verse reads, "When observing the mind, there is no mind, as it is empty of an entity." Having come to the previous realization, one reflects on the constitution of the mind and also comes to the conclusion that the mind itself has no enduring substance or essence. When the various elements of the mind are examined, the mind does not reveal itself as being a self-existing entity or as having superior reality to the external material world.

The third line in the verse reads, "When observing both, dualistic fixation is spontaneously freed." Having conducted these observations, the meditator looks at both the objective world and the subjective mind and examines the relationship between them. At this point, the meditator would develop appreciation for the fact that both the objective world, posited as existing by itself independent of the mind, and the subjective mind, posited as having some kind of self-sufficient existence of its own and thus being endowed with an enduring essence or substance, are products of conceptual construction.

The last line in the verse reads, "May we realize the natural state of the luminous mind." Rangjung Dorjé concludes with the wish that meditators are able to realize that the nature of the mind is luminosity. The nature of the mind, being all-encompassing, cannot be bifurcated. It cannot be divided into the domains of an objective world which exists independently of the mind and a subjective mind which also has some kind of self-subsistence.

Both this verse and the verse preceding it concentrate on the importance of developing insight as part of vipashyana meditation. This means that the way the mind is constituted has to be examined and the various elements and aspects of it analyzed. Not all Mahayana Buddhists agree on this, however. Some have said that the meditator should come to the realization of ultimate reality, not through analysis of the mind, but through analysis of the external material world. But, according to the Mahamudra tradition, it is through analysis of the mind that the meditator arrives at realization of the nature of the mind. This is not the only approach possible, but it is a more expedient way to secure that realization. This is borne out by statements found in various Mahayana sutras. For example, in the sutra known as *Enlightenment of Vairocana*,[33] it is said that a wise bodhisattva must engage in the practice of analysis of the mind, because it is through this analysis that they will come to the conclusion that the nature of the mind is devoid of obscurations and defilements. The nature of the mind is not vitiated by conceptual constructs or emotional conflicts.

For that reason, this type of practice is very important and should not be used as an adjunct to vipashyana meditation; it should constitute the *essential part* of vipashyana practice. Instead of using vipashyana practice to analyze the external material world through the use of logic, it is suggested that it is more profitable to analyze the constitution of the mind itself on the grounds that what the meditator experiences is more immediate. Even one's experience of the external world is determined by the way in which one's mind functions and the way in which it is constituted. So, in a way, it is not possible to understand the reality of the external world as it exists, totally independent of the mind. One cannot step outside one's experience of it. To do so would entail bypassing the mind, which is not possible.

If the mind is examined properly, in terms of its constitution, elements, and nature, then it is possible to attain enlightenment more directly. This point is made because the sutric Mahayana teachings contained in the Madhyamaka tradition and its subschools, emphasize the importance of first coming to realize the reality of the external world. They argue it is through that realization that one is able to secure enlightenment. But, according to the teachings of Mahamudra and the Mahayana teachings of the Yogacara school, it is the mind that should be used as the object of analysis. Through this analysis, the meditator arrives at the understanding of ultimate reality.

It should be pointed out, though, that analysis of the mind is not the goal of vipashyana meditation. Analysis is used in order to arrive at a correct conceptual understanding of the mind, but a full appreciation of the nature of the mind can be done only through contemplative, not analytical meditation. After having come to a correct conceptual notion of what the mind is, one should then engage in the contemplative method. While the analytical method should precede the contemplative method, both are necessary in order to develop insight. As has already been pointed out, to develop insight one needs three things—hearing or studying, analytical meditation, and contemplative meditation. The first two lead the meditator to the last stage of developing insight, which is contemplative meditation and that, in turn, secures enlightenment.

Although analytical practice is an important part of meditation, nevertheless, one should not think that what one realizes conceptually through such a practice is the Mahamudra experience. It is not Mahamudra experience because it is conceptual. Mahamudra experience is non-conceptual. However, conceptual apprehension is important as a prelude to genuine understanding of the Mahamudra experience, which is obtained through contemplative meditation.

Verse 19

> *Being free from mental fabrication, it is Mahamudra.*
> *Devoid of extremes, it is the Great Middle Way.*
> *It is also called Dzogchen, the embodiment of all.*
> *May we attain the confidence of realizing all by knowing one nature.*

This verse brings out the essence of both shamatha and vipashyana through emphasizing the unity of these two practices. The essence of Mahamudra is the state of non-fabrication. Another way of expressing it is to describe this state as being devoid of discursive thoughts. However, at this point it should be realized that what Mahamudra is saying is no different from the way in which ultimate reality has been described in the sutric or non-tantric teachings of Mahayana Buddhism. That approach, exemplified by the teachings of Madhyamaka or the school of the Middle way, describes reality as not falling into either the extreme of nihilism or that of eternalism.

In Dzogchen, also known as Maha Ati, ultimate reality is described as "self-effected." So, as a practitioner, it is important to realize how these different descriptions of reality do not, in fact, conflict. The same reality is being described and interpreted in different ways according to each of the traditions. That is why the last line in the verse states, "May we attain the confidence of realizing all by knowing one nature" while the previous three lines mention Mahamudra, the Middle Way, and Dzogchen. There can be only one ultimate reality. There can be only one nature of the mind. If one has the ability to realize the nature of reality or the nature of the mind, then one would naturally have realized all the others.

For this reason, Phakmo Drupa,[34] one of the great masters of the Kagyupa tradition, a disciple of Gampopa who, in turn, was the disciple of Milarepa, has said:

> Through the practice of Mahamudra, one is able to tame the conflicting emotions.
>
> Those teachings concerned with monastic discipline, the Vinaya, are therefore embodied within the practice of Mahamudra without the necessity of following the Vinaya teachings themselves.
>
> The Mahamudra teachings reveal how discursive thoughts can be used to realize dharmakaya, or the true nature of our being. The essential instructions of the tantric teachers are therefore embodied within the practice of Mahamudra.
>
> Through the Mahamudra teachings, one realizes all forms of extremes are to be avoided. The Mahamudra teachings therefore do not contradict the Madhyamaka system of Mahayana Buddhism. For this reason, a Mahamudra practitioner will develop the understanding that this is the essence of the teachings of Prajnaparamita or the wisdom sutras of Mahayana Buddhism.
>
> The Mahamudra practitioner understands that neither samsara nor nirvana transcend the realm of one's experience, and so apprehends the primacy of the mind. In doing so

they arrive at the knowledge that Dzogchen, Maha Ati, is not something different.

By not entertaining thoughts such as "this is a good experience," "that is a bad experience," one realizes Mahamudrahood. In keeping with the Shijé or Pacification tradition, the practice of Mahamudra has the capacity to pacify all forms of suffering.

Through Mahamudra practice, all forms of emotion and discursive thought are transformed so as to advance the practitioner on the spiritual path. The essence of the tantric teachings is therefore embodied within Mahamudra.

The Mahamudra teachings are in keeping with the teachings of what is known as the "tradition of co-emergent wisdom." Through this practice, the individual has the realization that discursive thoughts, dharmakaya and the mind are co-present and exist in harmonious relationship.

This exposition by Phakmo Drupa gives one an appreciation of how, through engaging in one particular practice, such as the method of Mahamudra, one is able to understand the very thing that all the other traditions are aiming at. There is no difference in the goal, in terms of what is to be realized. The methods used in the various traditions, and the terms employed to describe ultimate reality or the goal should not mislead the practitioner into thinking that people who follow these traditions are following different things, that they are trying to arrive at different goals. The aim of all these traditions is to assist the practitioner in understanding ultimate reality. It is possible to use the Mahamudra method and apprehend ultimate reality or use any of the other methods and realize the same thing in an indirect manner. The Mahayana sutra known as *Highest Continuum*,[34] for example, makes a similar point, saying that just as honey always has the same taste regardless of how it is used to sweeten different types of delicacies, so, too, all the varieties of teachings of Buddhism have the same intention. This intention is to lead the individual practitioner to enlightenment and this entails the apprehension of ultimate reality.

Sometimes the Mahamudra technique is known as *karpo chik thup* in Tibetan, which means something like "panacea," one medicine with the ability to cure all diseases. Having said that, the follower of the Mahamudra tradition should bear another point in mind, and this has to do with the idea of non-mentation or remaining in a state where there is no mental fabrication. Certain people have objected to this type of practice, saying that if the meditator attempts to secure a state of mind where there is no thought-flow whatsoever, and enters into a state of total nothingness or voidness, this will distract them from securing a real state of meditation, because Buddhist meditation places emphasis on awareness, not on absorption or trance.

In response, it should be made clear that a state of non-fabrication does not mean entering into a state of non-thought or nothingness or inducing a form of trance. Instead, it means that the meditator should let go of everything that arises in the mind. In Sanskrit this state is called *amanasikara*; "a" meaning "non" and *manasikara* meaning "mentation"—so, "non-mentation" or "non-thought." However, within the Mahamudra teachings, this word can be understood in a unique way. The "a," which is the negative particle in the word, can signify ultimate reality; so "a" then means "that which is originless, non-created, non-differentiated." It therefore means "emptiness." Manasikara then, can be interpreted to mean "not getting fixated on that which is uncreated, unoriginated, and remaining instead without attachment, without clinging." In brief, amanasikara or *yila mijepa* in Tibetan, basically means "letting go." It has nothing to do with trying to produce a mental state comparable to a total state of blankness, where there is nothing happening in the mind.

The sutra on Manjushri, for example, says, "The letter 'a' is the supreme of all letters, because it signifies ultimate reality. It signifies that which is not created, is unoriginated and inexpressible." A similar point has been made in the tantric text known as *Hevajra*,[35] a very important tantric text. Here, it says, "The letter 'a' refers to ultimate reality and, through an understanding of that, one is able to secure enlightenment." In relation to the word "amanasikara" then, while "a" is normally understood as the negative particle in a word, in this particular context "a" can be interpreted to mean or refer to ultimate reality. "To remain in a state of non-fabrication" means to remain in a natural state of mind, a state which is emptiness itself, without being fixated on that state but, rather, being able to let it go. Therefore, "non-fabrication" does not mean "non-thought" as in the ordinary sense.

These references to different texts, both from the sutras and the tantras, are made in order to draw textual support for the Mahamudra notion of "non-thought" or "non-mentation" because, as has been pointed out, certain people have expressed reservations regarding the genuineness of Mahamudra experience, particularly when it comes to this emphasis on the state of non-fabrication.

The experience of Mahamudra leads to the state of non-fabrication, but the word "Mahamudra" can have different meanings. Mostly "mudra" means "not going beyond;" in Tibetan it is called *chakya*. "Not going beyond" refers to the fact that Mahamudra is all-encompassing; there is nothing left out, in terms of samsara or nirvana. *Maha* in Sanskrit means "great." This is *chenpo* in Tibetan, meaning that there is nothing greater. When it is said in this context that there is nothing greater, this should be understood in relation to the practice of tantric Buddhism. Generally in tantric Buddhism, three types of mudra are mentioned—karmamudra, jnanamudra, and Mahamudra. "Maha" signifies that Mahamudra is superior to the other two. In tantric Buddhist practice, karmamudra is used as part of sexual yoga, which aims to transmute sexuality into spiritual practice. Jnanamudra entails visualization of male and female deities in sexual union. Mahamudra does not deal with either of these, but instead deals directly with the nature of the mind and ultimate reality. For this reason, it is called "great" because it is superior to the other two mudras. This point has been made in the text known in Tibetan as *Kandrel Pemachen*,[36] which says that karmamudra and jnanamudra, as practiced within the tantric tradition, still deal with various experiences of the individual in the samsaric condition, whereas the Mahamudra method goes beyond that.

For this reason, Mahamudra is superior to both the other mudras. Sometimes, certain tantric practitioners have objected to such an approach. They argue that one cannot be a tantric practitioner and practice Mahamudra if one has not been first initiated into the other two mudras; that one cannot go straight into Mahamudra practice. In response to that it can be said that it is not always necessary to go through such a step-by-step process; it is possible to engage in Mahamudra practice without first having practiced the other two mudras. As the *Wheel of Time* says, "A real practitioner should try to rise above the practice of karmamudra and jnanamudra and engage in the practice of Mahamudra." Furthermore, it goes on to say that in order to transcend one's sexual desire one should engage in karmamudra; in order to understand the nature of the mind one should practice jnanamudra; and in order to understand ultimate reality one should practice Mahamudra.

Verse 20

Great bliss, free from attachment, is unceasing.
Luminosity, devoid of fixation, is unobscured.
Non-thought, transcending the intellect, is spontaneously present.
Without effort, may our experience be unceasing.

As the meditator proceeds with the practice of tranquility and insight along the lines of the Mahamudra tradition, three different types of meditative experience are expected to arise. It should be noted that there is a considerable difference between meditative experience and meditative realization. This particular verse describes only meditative experience, not meditative realization. The first of these experiences is the experience of bliss. Bliss arises when grasping and clinging have ceased to operate in the mind. Feelings of frustration, discontent, and dissatisfaction have their origin in the mind's propensity to latch onto things without being able to let go, so when the meditator is able to let go of things, the experience of bliss naturally arises.

The second experience of meditation is the experience of luminosity. Luminosity manifests as a consequence of increased mental clarity. It comes from not being fixated on sensory impressions. The meditator does not view what is presented to the senses as having objective, self-sufficient reality. Viewing sensory impressions as having substantial, independent reality is what causes confusion in the mind and, hence, the dimming of mental clarity. The third experience is that of non-conceptuality. This comes from having a certain insight into ultimate reality or emptiness, because ultimate reality is not grasped through conceptual categories.

Although these three types of meditative experience are expected to arise at one time or another, either together or individually, nevertheless, the meditator should not be too concerned about them. In other words, the meditator should not be lured into reacting with either hope or fear. They should not be hoping for the perpetuation of these experiences if they have arisen or, if they have not arisen, that they have such experiences. They should also not fear they will be incapable of inducing the experiences or sustaining them over a long period of time, or that they will lose them. Rather than reacting in these ways, the meditator must cultivate an open attitude towards the varieties of experience that may arise during meditation.

The key point is for the meditator to let the mind be in its own natural state, allowing whatever experiences there are in the mind to arise, and to be present. It is not only unnecessary but, in fact, may be harmful to exercise conscious effort to try to bring about certain states of mind or to create a particular state of mind during meditation. To do these things is anathema to the Mahamudra approach to meditation, which is the natural approach rather than a manufactured one. Furthermore, if the meditator does not deal with these experiences properly, then the experiences themselves can become corrupted. For example, having the experience of bliss could very easily lead to attachment to that experience. Luminosity too may become corrupted by fixating on it. A similar kind of corruption can also occur in relation to the experience of emptiness or ultimate reality, because subsequent to having such an experience one may try to make sense of it through the application of conceptual categories.

In brief, meditators should always exercise an element of caution. If they feel dissatisfied through not having had these experiences, they may try to induce them through deliberate effort, which may end up misleading them. If one has had an experience, one may also want to hang onto it and not be able to let go. Either way, these situations present obstacles. So, applying the first approach of deliberately trying to bring about certain kinds of experience presents an obstacle to having such experiences. If the second approach is applied, then even if one has had certain meditative experiences, they will not endure, simply because one is trying too hard to maintain or sustain the experience. One is trying to prolong it through conscious effort. It is absolutely essential, therefore, that the meditator does not try to do either of these but, in fact, makes no conscious effort to bring about such experiences. Instead, one should attempt to let the mind be in its natural state. The verse concludes by wishing that the meditator continues to have such experiences without obstacles.

When bliss is spoken about in this context, this does not simply refer to either physical bliss or mental bliss, but to both. A sense of well-being has to permeate both the physical and mental dimensions. "Luminosity" means that the mind at that point is free from the two fundamental obstacles to meditation, namely mental agitation and stupor, so there is a sense of clarity. "Non-conceptuality" simply means that when the mind has become completely settled and there is that sense of mental clarity, one is led to the perception of emptiness or ultimate reality. If the meditator develops the skill to deal properly with these various experiences, as mentioned earlier, and does not become attached to them or try to produce them through deliberate effort, this will lead to the experience of the non-divisibility of bliss and emptiness. In other words, it will lead to the merging of these three experiences, which are all higher meditative states attained by the yogis. These will occur naturally.

As for the mechanism involved in how these experiences come about, this is very simple. When the mind becomes free of agitation, the psychophysical flow of energy is modified. When that happens, it creates the appropriate physical and mental state for the meditative experiences to occur. Being in that mental and physical state leads to the experience of bliss; bliss leads to mental clarity; and mental clarity leads to non-conceptuality. When the meditator progresses along the path and becomes skilled in terms of dealing with these experiences, all three types of meditative experience will be non-differentiated. That leads to realization. So, first the meditator has to experience these things and then, through those experiences, they are able to secure realization. Once realization is attained, of course, the experience of bliss, and so on, become more permanent and enduring, rather than transient, as is normally the case with meditative experiences.

Verse 21

> *The fixation of clinging to good experiences is*
>   *spontaneously freed.*
> *The confusion of "bad thoughts" is naturally purified.*
> *Ordinary mind is free from acceptance and rejection.*
> *May we realize the truth of dharmata, devoid of*
>   *constructs.*

As the previous verse pointed out, the meditator must not develop attachment towards positive experiences during meditation. For example, if one is able to enter quite naturally into a state of calmness and tranquility, one would not view that as something so wonderful that it has to be maintained at all costs. The meditator should adopt the same attitude towards other experiences in meditation, such as clarity and bliss. When the meditator has this attitude, the attachment to positive experiences naturally dissipates or becomes self-liberated. In other words, the meditator does not need to use a specific method or apply an antidote to overcome attachment. The attachment is naturally self-liberated.

It is not only in relation to positive experiences during meditation that the meditator needs to cultivate this attitude; it also applies to negative experiences. Experiences of mental disturbance which include agitation, restlessness, and distraction, are brought about by conflicting emotions and conceptual confusion. The same attitude of equanimity is then maintained toward these mental disturbances, so instead of applying specific methods to get rid of them, they will disappear within the natural state of the mind. This does not mean that mental disturbances should not be overcome. The meditator has to overcome them, but they are not overcome by relying on antidotes, methods, or techniques of controlling the mind. For this reason, it is said that the confusion of bad thoughts is naturally purified. According to Mahamudra teachings, one does not have to accept or cultivate the various states of mind which, spiritually speaking, one may regard as positive or beneficial, or reject and discard thoughts and emotions which one may feel are non-beneficial or disruptive. The meditator should go beyond notions of acceptance and rejection regarding their experiences.

This is borne out by the third line in the verse, "Ordinary mind is free from acceptance and rejection." When the meditator does not deliberately cultivate positive states of mind, both emotional and conceptual, or reject negative states of mind, they will be able to remain in the state of what is called "ordinary mind." "Ordinary mind," here, refers to the mind as a whole, where the meditator is not entertaining thoughts of acceptance and rejection but, rather, is able to remain with a sense of awareness and attentiveness. In this way, the mind is not conditioned by preconceived notions about what it is to be in the meditative state.

Due to various notions about what the meditative state is like, people often get caught up in ideas about what that state is and then try to seek the meditative state that they think should be cultivated. Other states of mind experienced during meditation are then seen as disruptive and perceived as the cause of various obstacles to the development of that idealized meditative state and therefore something to be discarded or rejected. When these thoughts are not entertained, and the mind is allowed to rest, one can remain in the state of ordinary mind regardless of the experiences one is having at any given moment. The reason this is so is because in terms of the nature or essence of the mind, there is no difference between a mind that is disturbed and a mind that is at rest and imbued with a sense of tranquility. The nature of the mind can be realized through mental agitation as much as through the state of tranquility or mind at rest, provided the meditator can exercise a sense of awareness and let the mind be, without contrivance.

This is not so very different from what the sutric teachings have to say about the nature of phenomena and the external world. As the *Heart Sutra*[37] says, "Form is not different from emptiness, and emptiness is not different from form." In a similar way, the nature of the mind is not different from the various mental states and experiences—good and bad, wholesome and unwholesome, encouraging and frustrating. The great Kagyupa masters have pointed out that the mind in its natural state is totally free from any concept of acceptance and rejection, and the nature of the mind can be perceived or realized only through this method, this being, in fact, not applying a specific method to control the mind. These past masters realized that even the notion of using antidotes to produce certain meditative states and prevent other mental states from arising is a part of the mental disturbances that the meditator has to overcome.

The key point is not to become caught up with that but, rather, to allow the mind to be, so that the disturbances naturally dissipate. This enables the ordinary mind to emerge of its own accord. If this attitude is developed, then all the various distractions that may be brought about through sensory impressions, emotional upheaval, and conceptual confusion dissipate like the clouds in the sky—not vanishing due to an external cause, but of their own accord. Various sutric teachings are given for beginners, of course, explaining how to control the passions and emotions. These include techniques to employ in order to develop positive qualities and to control the negative propensities in the mind and in one's behavior. The practitioner of Mahamudra, however, should go beyond this, beyond any notion of acceptance and rejection.

The verse is summed up in the last line: "May we realize the truth of dharmata, devoid of constructs." To expand this a little, here Rangjung Dorjé is saying, "May the meditator realize dharmata or the nature of the mind, the ordinary mind, which is free from constructs." Any notion of acceptance or rejection is part of the conceptual constructs which have to be abandoned. However, they are not abandoned by using specific methods but through the use of no method, and that is simply to let the mind be in its natural state.

Verse 22

The nature of all beings is always the enlightened state.
But, not realizing it, they wander endlessly in samsara.
Towards the countless sentient beings who suffer,
May overwhelming compassion arise in our minds.

Having described how the view should be established and the manner in which the meditator should practice meditation, the text supplements this with the notion or concept of compassion. Without compassion, the meditator may enjoy a certain element of quietude and to some extent may, in fact, develop wisdom. It is not possible, though, to become fully realized. The element of compassion is essential to becoming fully realized. Compassion is described in two stages. Firstly, compassion has to be identified and then must be explained in relation to emptiness or ultimate reality. This verse is concerned with the idea of determining what sort of compassion is spoken about in this context.

Within Mahayana Buddhism, three different types of compassion are described. There is compassion that arises in relation to sentient creatures; compassion that manifests as a response to existing things as a whole; and compassion that can arise without any referent whatsoever. The first two types of compassion should accompany one's preliminary practices, in relation to the Mahamudra tradition. The compassion referred to in this particular verse, however, is the third type. This type of compassion can only arise when ultimate reality has been apprehended. It is normally described as "compassion without intention" or "compassion without referent."

This compassion is demonstrated as a result of having established the right view, as described in the previous sections of the prayer. As this verse tells us, "The nature of all beings is always the enlightened state." All living sentient beings possess buddha nature, which is uncorrupted, translucent, and unvitiated, and therefore the nature of sentient beings is no different from the authentic aspect of buddha's being. Due to ignorance, however, sentient beings do not have this knowledge or insight. For this reason, they wander about in the samsaric condition and experience various forms of suffering and dissatisfaction. When the meditator comes in contact with these beings, compassion arises but this time compassion arises quite naturally, as a result of having had insight into the nature of reality. As Nagarjuna, the founder of Madhyamaka philosophy has said, "If the meditator uses emptiness as the object of meditation often enough, the natural inclination to benefit others will arise without any doubt." The bodhisattvas and meditators who have had that insight into ultimate reality do not need to deliberately produce compassion; it arises as a natural consequence of having developed insight.

This particular verse, then, identifies the nature of compassion and, in relation to the three types of compassion presented in the Mahayana teachings, it is the last type of compassion that is being described. The most supreme of all compassionate experiences is the compassion that manifests only when one has had insight into the nature of reality.

The message of the next verse has already been described, in that compassion and emptiness or compassion and ultimate reality should be seen in unity, as there is no difference between the wisdom that leads to realization of emptiness and the development of compassion.

Verse 23

> *The play of overwhelming compassion being unobstructed,*
> *In the moment of love the empty essence nakedly dawns.*
> *May we constantly practice, day and night,*
> *This supreme path of unity, devoid of errors.*

When this compassion without intention or referent arises and there is love for others, this type of emotional experience does not degenerate into mere sentimentality. It is sustained by the understanding of the nature of things, of how things exist. It is not corrupted by various conceptual categories or frames of reference. The nature of the experience of these beings is direct and immediate and therefore non-conceptual, for it is not reliant upon any concept of universals. In this way, emptiness and compassion are experienced as having the same flavor; they are experienced as unity. If one is able to pursue one's practice in this manner then the path becomes free of error and deviation.

The *Diamond Pinnacle Tantra*,[38] for example, says, "The real essence of compassion cannot be separated from emptiness or ultimate reality." Trying to separate compassion from emptiness is like trying to separate luminosity from the flame of a lamp. When the non-divisibility of emptiness and compassion is talked about, one should try to understand it in relation to luminosity and the flame of a lamp and the nature of their inseparability. The ultimate reality that is emptiness is realized through wisdom, and wisdom is no different from compassion. Sometimes it is said that wisdom is emptiness, and skillful means or method is compassion, so the meditator should always try to cultivate both. One should cultivate wisdom in order to gain greater insight into emptiness and cultivate compassion in order to develop one's skills in relation to dealing with others. There should be no bias of one against the other.

Even the tantric teachings such as *Guhyasamaja tantra*[39] say that a yogi should not exclusively rely on either the method, compassion, or on wisdom, but must pursue the practice of the union of these two. Furthermore, in a sutra known as *Questions of the Naga King Anavatapta*, it is stated that a meditator is liable to fall into two different types of pitfall. One is to invest all one's energy solely into the development of compassion and cultivate the skills to benefit others. The other is to think only of developing wisdom at the expense of compassionate activities. These two types of pitfall must be avoided. Atisha, the prominent master of the Kadampa tradition, also says that anyone who thinks of simply cultivating either compassion or wisdom exclusively will only be led to bondage, not liberation. The *Ornament of Realization*[40] says that if the meditator cultivates only wisdom, they will not dwell in the samsaric condition. If, at the same time, compassion is cultivated however, then that person would not dwell in nirvana either. In this way, the Mahayana practitioner, or any realized being, for that matter, is able to simultaneously avoid the suffering of samsara and the quietude of nirvana.

There are many more teachings that emphasize this point, so it is important to see how compassion and wisdom, or compassion and emptiness, must not be pursued separately but simultaneously. If a meditator has not cultivated wisdom and has no idea what ultimate reality is, then even if that person tries to do something good for the benefit of others this will be only of limited benefit. It will not have the benefit that could have been obtained had one invested time and energy into developing insight. It is very easy for such a person to abandon the pursuit of wisdom as a result of experiences of overwhelming emotional content—for example, becoming too sentimentally involved with the object of one's compassion and thus discarding all spiritual practices save the cultivation of compassion. Ultimately, pursuing compassion in this manner can only be an obstacle, rather than a liberating factor. The same has to be said regarding the practice or cultivation of wisdom. If wisdom is cultivated without any thought given to the importance of compassion, it is very easy for the meditator to become self-engrossed. In doing so, the meditator becomes caught up in the various inner experiences brought about by these practices, without gaining realization.

Therefore, both the inner and outer aspects of the meditator's practice are essential in order to attain buddhahood. Outwardly, the meditator has to practice love and compassion in relation to other beings. Inwardly they should cultivate wisdom. The greater the wisdom, however, the greater is one's corresponding ability to show compassion towards others in an intelligent and skillful manner. Rangjung Dorjé concludes the verse by requesting that the meditator combines these two practices and meditates on this day and night, until achieving enlightenment.

Additional remarks

A few further points can be made regarding the previous verses. For example, the verse that talks about the meditative experience of bliss actually describes what are called the "path of accumulation" and the "path of application" in Mahayana Buddhism. The verses that talk about realization from then onwards, including the present and previous verses, point out the essential practices of the "path of seeing" and the "path of meditation."

In relation to what is called "view, meditation, and action," a lot has been said thus far about the view and meditation but not much has been said about action. This changes when we come to these two verses in the prayer. Some people might say, "Well, action is not really emphasized; it is only the view and meditation that are emphasized in this prayer." That, however, is a misunderstanding. According to Mahamudra and tantric teachings, two types of action are described. One is the *external* aspect of action and the other is the *internal* one. The external aspect has to do with the taking of various precepts, and trying to determine the right thing to do—what sorts of actions should be followed through and what sorts of actions should be refrained from. The internal aspect has to do with mental acts, the meditator's attitudes, beliefs, and various mental states.

According to Mahamudra teachings, it is not the external form of action that is the most important; rather, it is the inner acts of the mind, the mental acts. If the meditator has been able to gain sufficient understanding of the view and meditation, the external aspect of actions naturally follows. In that way, one should not think that the aspect of action has been ignored in this prayer, with greater emphasis given to view and meditation. Even developing view and meditation is a form of action. If one has been able to develop the correct view and has meditated in the way described in the prayer, appropriate action will naturally follow. This is not only the view of Mahamudra; Tantrism as a whole promotes the same view.

Section Six

Fruition

Verse 24

> *The eyes and superknowledges resulting from the power of practice,*
> *The ripening of sentient beings, the cultivation of buddha realms,*
> *And the perfection of aspirations to accomplish all enlightened qualities—*
> *May we attain the buddhahood of having accomplished ripening, cultivation and perfection.*

Having now covered the path, the prayer's concluding verse deals with the fruition. This verse is explained in two stages. The first stage involves explication of the content, while the second stage makes certain remarks regarding the path and fruition.

When the meditator has pursued the practice over a period of time, that person will go through the various stages of experience and realization, which will lead eventually to enlightenment or buddhahood. When buddhahood is attained, the meditator is endowed with various qualities, such as supernormal perception and psychic ability. The reason one possesses these extraordinary qualities is because of the eradication of defilements and obscurations of the mind. Consequently, the senses become heightened so the person's sight, hearing, and so on, become extremely acute.

Concurrent with these heightened senses, the enlightened being develops various psychic abilities, powers of the mind not previously present. This does not mean, however, that these powers are not evident while the meditator is undertaking the journey. They are evident but the nature of these powers is that they are developmental and progressive. It is only with attainment of full realization or enlightenment that these qualities become complete. For this reason, the verse says, "The eyes and superknowledges resulting from the power of practice..."

The verse goes on to describe the other qualities of enlightenment: "The ripening of sentient beings, the cultivation of buddha realms and the perfection of aspirations to accomplish all enlightened qualities." The bodhisattva or meditator begins to have intimations of such powers while on the path and their cultivation of right attitude, right aspiration, and engaging in right activity, in combination, helps to foster development of these powers.

The bodhisattvas and enlightened beings, such as the Buddha, are able to do three things. The first is ripening sentient beings, the second is cultivation of buddha fields, and the third is perfection of aspiration.

The first of these three, "the ripening of sentient beings" is likened to the ripening of fruit. If the fruit itself does not have the capacity to mature then even if the right sorts of external conditions are present, the ripening process will not take place. In a similar way, sentient beings already have the ability to become enlightened. Therefore, it is possible for the bodhisattvas and buddhas, the enlightened beings, to help with that process. Similarly, even if a fruit seed has the ability to germinate and grow and eventually mature into a fully-grown fruit tree, without the right soil, an irrigation system, and a farmer attending to it, the seed will be lost. Therefore, even though sentient beings have that innate capacity to become awakened, there is still the need for the kindness and compassion of bodhisattvas and buddhas, in order for that process of ripening or maturity to be effected.

The second one, "the cultivation of buddha fields" means that when the mind is devoid of conceptual distortion and emotional conflict, when there is total clarity and perspicacity of the mind then whatever one experiences is seen as pure. Everything is seen as a buddha field. This is sometimes referred to as "pure perception." Another term used for the cultivation of buddha fields is "purification." The reason sentient beings normally see things as being undesirable, ugly, and depressing has to do with the inner workings of the mind rather than the nature of things as such. These sorts of qualities or properties of the enlightened mind are explained by Asanga in his *Bodhisattvabhumi*.[41]

The third one is "the perfection of aspiration." "Aspiration," in this context, is like praying—praying that things will turn out for the better, just like this Mahamudra prayer, with its wish that sentient beings become enlightened and that the meditator has the appropriate experiences. Aspiration, from this point of view, has an intrinsic power so that, once the aspiration is made and followed up with practice, it takes on its own momentum and the aspiration becomes realized at the time of enlightenment, which is the perfection of aspiration.

The result of the perfection of aspiration is to actualize all the qualities or properties of an enlightened being, both physically and mentally. Physically, the body becomes transformed. We are not just referring to the body as one of the five skandhas[42] or psychophysical constituents, but to the body which becomes transformed into nirmanakaya. This means the body is no longer influenced by karmic imprints and is therefore pure. Mentally, as a result of having abandoned all the obscurations and defilements of the mind, two different types of wisdom become actualized: the wisdom that enables one to apprehend the nature of things, which is absolute truth, and the wisdom that apprehends the extent of things, or relative truth.

Having had insight into the five poisons—desire, anger, jealousy, pride, and ignorance—the five types of wisdom become actualized: mirror-like wisdom, wisdom of equanimity, wisdom of discrimination, wisdom of all-accomplishing action, and wisdom of the ultimate truth. With actualization of the full physical and mental potential, it is possible for the bodhisattva to work for the benefit of others. Such a being has the quality of having abandoned all impediments in the way of self-realization and working towards the benefit of others. Therefore, enlightened activity can be carried on and then become spontaneous. It is "spontaneous" in the sense of not being conditioned by karmic propensities and habits of the mind. Enlightened activity is also unceasing. Because it is spontaneous and not conditioned by karmic patterns, there is never a time when such a being is not benefitting others.

To say one has arrived at the goal, the end of the journey, the terminus, is to say that one has become enlightened. That is called "*Buddha*" in Sanskrit and *sangyé* in Tibetan. Buddha basically means "awakened." *Sang* means "abandoned." Simply put, "abandonment of ignorance." *Gye* means "expansion" or "flowering," and this is "the flowering of insight." This state is attained when the bodhisattva has been able to accomplish the three types of activity mentioned previously—ripening, purification, and perfection, with perfection leading directly to the realization of perfect, complete enlightenment. No matter what type of path one follows, whether it is from the sutric point of view or the tantric point of view, the bodhisattva or meditator has to go through these stages of accomplishment. Rangjung Dorjé concludes the verse by saying, "May we attain the buddhahood of having accomplished such ripening, cultivation and perfection."

That concludes the description of the content of this verse. In addition to that, however, something can be said regarding how path and fruition, the path and attainment of buddhahood can be understood within the context of the Mahamudra tradition of practice. It has often been said that Mahamudra does not rely so much on the idea of path, particularly a path which involves various paths and stages, as has been described in the Mahayana tradition of practice. As a result, some people may wonder if there is any conflict between the Mahamudra and Mahayana approaches. According to the Mahamudra masters, there is no conflict between the teachings of the graded path, as described in sutric Mahayana teachings, and the direct, pointing-out instructions of Mahamudra, because in the Mahamudra teachings we speak about "four yogas."

The first one is the yoga of one-pointedness. The yoga of one-pointedness is realized when the meditator has the experience of concentration combined with insight. At that point, the meditator may experience bliss, non-conceptuality, and luminosity or clarity of the mind.

The second yoga is the yoga of non-conceptuality, which is realized when the meditator sees everything from the point of view of bliss. Whatever the meditator experiences, whether internally or brought about through external means, through sensory impressions, the mind is not disturbed. This is basically the genuine experience of the meditation of insight.

The third yoga is the yoga of one flavor which comes about when the realization of the yoga of non-conceptuality becomes deepened. Instead of the dichotomies, the dualities dominating the mind—pain and pleasure, happiness and unhappiness, samsara and nirvana, internal mind and external physical world—everything is seen as having the same flavor, the flavor of ultimate reality.

The final yoga is the yoga of non-meditation, which is the same as the attainment of buddhahood. This is realized when the meditator comes to experience that the mental clarity, developed through meditation practice, is non-differentiable from the innate quality of wakefulness in the mind. The reason the fourth yoga is known as "yoga of non-meditation" is because when enlightenment has been secured, there is no distinction between what is experienced during meditation and what is experienced in post-meditation situations.

Each of the four yogas can be divided into three stages—small, middling, and advanced. If we compare the sutric teachings of the Mahayana path and the four yogas of Mahamudra, we can discern a parallel there. The three stages of one-pointed yoga and the first two stages of the yoga of non-conceptuality correspond to the path of accumulation. The advanced level of the yoga of non-conceptuality corresponds to the path of seeing. The first stage of the yoga of one flavor, through to the intermediary level of non-meditation, corresponds to what is known as the path of meditation, according to the sutric teachings. The advanced level of non-meditation is the attainment of buddhahood. So through this comparison one gains the understanding that approaching enlightenment using the Mahamudra method is not in conflict with the approach of the more conventional sutric Mahayana tradition.

Verse 25

> *By the power of the compassion of the victorious ones*
> *and their sons and daughters in the ten directions*
> *And by all the perfect virtue that exists,*
> *May I and all beings attain accomplishment in*
> *accordance with these aspirations*

The final verse in Karmapa Rangjung Dorjé's *The Aspiration of the Mahamudra of True Meaning*, is the dedication, the wish that all beings attain realization through this aspiration. That concludes the text, *The Song of Karmapa: The Aspiration of the Mahamudra of True Meaning*.

Notes

Editor's Introduction

1. *Shamatha*: Shamatha meditation is also referred to as tranquility meditation and calm abiding. The main purpose of shamatha meditation is to relax and stabilize the mind by using a unitary focus such as the breath to allow the activity of the mind to settle. This is done for the primary purpose of preparing the mind to practice vipashyana or insight meditation. The practice of shamatha meditation is common to most schools of Buddhism.

2. *Vipashyana*: Vipashyana meditation, also known as "analytical meditation." It uses a range of techniques to build insight into how the mind works and the nature of reality.

3. *Dohas*: Spontaneous songs of realization that came directly from the mahasiddha's own experiences and contained direct instructions for meditation and realization.

4. *Maitreya* (ca. 270-350 CE): One of the three founders of the Yogacara school of Buddhist philosophy, along with Asanga and Vasubandhu. Some scholars believe this Maitreya to be a historical person in India. The traditions themselves have held that it is referring to Maitreya, the future buddha

5. *Asanga*: Founder of the Yogacara school along with his half-brother Vasubandhu. He reputedly received these teachings from Maitreya, the future Buddha, in Tushita heaven.

6. *Ü*: A province in Tibet which together with Tsang, forms central Tibet, Ü-tsang, one of the three regions of Tibet, the other two being Kham and Amdo.

7. *Kalachakra*: "Wheel of Time" or "Cycles of Time." The Kalachakra tradition revolves around the concept of time (*kala*) and cycles (*chakra*): from the cycles of the planets, to the cycles of human breathing, it teaches the practice of working with the most subtle energies within one's body on the path to enlightenment. It is one of the Anuttarayoga Tantras, the highest of four classes of tantra in the Sarma or new schools of Tibetan Buddhism.

8. *Chö*: A practice found primarily in the Nyingma and Kagyü schools of Tibetan Buddhism and based on the Prajna paramita or "Perfection of Wisdom" sutras. It is also known as "Cutting Through," meaning "To Cut Through the Ego."

9. *The five standard topics of a monastic curriculum:*

    Pramana: Means "proof" and "means of knowledge." It refers to epistemology, the theory of knowledge and encompasses one or more reliable and valid means by which human beings gain accurate, true knowledge. The focus of Pramana is how correct knowledge can be acquired, how one knows, how one doesn't, and to what extent knowledge pertinent about someone or something can be acquired.

    Prajnaparamita: The "Perfection of Wisdom," or more literally, "transcendent wisdom." It refers to this perfected way of seeing the nature of reality, as well as to a particular body of sutras and to the personification of the concept of the Bodhisattva. Prajnaparamita is a central concept in Mahayana Buddhism and is generally associated with the doctrine of emptiness. Its practice and understanding are taken to be indispensable elements of the Bodhisattva path.

    Madhyamaka: Literally meaning "the middle way." One of the main schools of Mahayana Buddhism, it was founded by Nagarjuna and Aryadeva and emphasizes the doctrine of emptiness. The middle way describes the position taken by its adherents in relation to the existence or non-existence of things. Madhyamaka uses elaborate reasoning to prove that things do not have any enduring essence.

Abhidharmakosha: *Verses on the Treasury of Abhidharma*, composed by Vasubandhu in the 4th or 5th century and is a complete and systematic account of the Abhidharma.

Vinaya: one of the three pitakas or collections of the Buddhist scriptures, concerned primarily with monastic discipline.

10. *Dzogchen Nyingtik*: The innermost secret teachings of Dzogchen. Within the Dzogchen teachings, there are three categories of teachings suitable to students of different capacity. The Nyingtik is the innermost secret cycle of teachings and is the most direct approach for students of the highest capacity.

The Verses

11. With respect to the original translation being referenced throughout this book, the first verse stated only "sons," but at the discretion of the editor "sons" has been replaced with "sons and daughters." The spelling of certain words in Erik Pema Kunsang's tanslation have been changed to comply with US spelling.

Section One

12. The material for this book was taken from Traleg Rinpoche's oral commentary on the root verses by Rangjung Dorjé. Traleg Rinpoche based his talks on the traditional Tibetan commentary to the root verses by Situ Tenpai Nyinje (1700-1777), *Oral Transmission of the Supreme Siddhas*. The full title of this text in Wylie transliteration is: *nges don phyag rgya chen po'i smon lam gyi 'grel pa grub pa mchog gi zhal lung*, a detailed

translation of which may be found in Peter Roberts, *Mahamudra and Related Instructions: Core Teachings of the Kagyü Schools* (Boston: Wisdom Publications, 2011), pp 175-288.

13. In the context of Mahamudra teachings, we are not praying to an external supernatural being. Our objective is also not to receive what could be described as "grace" in response to our prayer. We are not motivated by the desire for redemption or any kind of favor from an external being. The Mahamudra prayer is oriented towards gathering and concentrating all of our psychic energy and projecting that into the future in the form of ideals and images. These personify what we would like to become. This is the objective and fundamental function of the prayer and is what the Tibetan term *mönlam* refers to. The term, while translated as prayer, has nothing to do with anything like asking for favors; it has no connotation of petition.

14. *Questions of the Naga King Anavatapta*: A sutra in which the Buddha explains to a naga king and an assembly of monks that reciting the four seals is equivalent to recitation of all of the 84,000 articles of the Dharma. He urges them to make diligent efforts to engage in understanding the four seals, which are the defining philosophical tenets of the Buddhist doctrine. The four seals are: all compounded phenomena are impermanent; all contaminated phenomena are suffering; all phenomena are without self; and nirvana is peace.

15. *Twenty Vows*: Also known as *Twenty Verses on the Bodhisattva Vow*. A short, clear, and simple account of the Bodhisattva vows written by Candragomin, an Indian lay practitioner of the 7th century, famous for his extensive learning and practice.

16. *Chandrakirti* (600-650): Abbot of Nalanda University and the

disciple of Nagarjuna, best known for the *Entering the Middle Way*, a commentary on Nagarjuna's major work. The founder of the Prasangika division of Madhyamaka philosophy.

17. *Entering the Middle Way*: Chandrakirti's classic commentary on the meaning of Nagarjuna's *Fundamental Verses on the Middle Way*. It is included among the so-called "thirteen great texts," which form the core of the curriculum in most monasteries.

18. *The six paramitas* or transcendental actions are practices used to reduce and relieve our suffering. They are the practice of: generosity, patience, moral precepts (see above in note 6), vigor, meditative concentration, and wisdom. The development of a spontaneous and open mind is seen as the basis for the growth of a fundamental sense of generosity. Generosity can be expressed materially, through seeking to give without expectations of a return; through seeking to protect those who are vulnerable; and through the skillfully imparting the Dharma. Patience is seen as the antidote to anger, frustration, resentment, hostility, and the like. One can actively work on patience to provide a more positive and unconditional inner environment. Vigor points to the importance of applying enthusiasm, energy, and maintaining motivation on one's spiritual journey to progress the immediate goal of self improvement, and the ultimate goal of enlightenment. The development of meditative concentration is seen as key to developing self understanding and thus progressing on the spiritual path. When meditation is practiced skillfully, one develops both wisdom and compassion. Wisdom provides insight into the sentient, and more specifically the human condition as well as the nature of reality. Here when we speak of reality, it refers to the insubstantial and transient nature of all things, and the interdependence of all things. So it is

proposed that when we investigate the mind through insight or analytical meditations, we are able to refine our understanding of how the mind works and how we relate to the world as samsaric beings. The samsaric tendency is to see things as, or desire things to be, static or at least self-serving. That is, serve our comfort and desire for happiness. Recognizing the cycle nature of "desire for" and "dissatisfaction with" our experiences sets up an ongoing cycle of grasping and fixation. Thus by observing how the mind works and what compels us to seek happiness leads to an ongoing state of dissatisfaction and suffering. Insight into these habitual compulsions and their causes is considered part of the process of gaining wisdom into the tendency we have to perpetuate samsara. As these realizations deepen, from a Mahayana perspective, one seeks to not only free oneself from this samsaric bondage but first seeks to free others from this bondage. One's spiritual journey focuses on the desire to reach enlightenment for the benefit of all sentient beings. The development of compassion provides an opportunity to act in the world with this wisdom and understanding in a way that can benefit others. Both the development of wisdom (insight into the nature of reality, and sentient and the human condition) and compassion (the act of seeking to provide whatever is essential to assist other beings) is seen as the greatest outcome from a practitioner's point of view. So training in the six paramitas provides the opportunity to develop essential qualities on the Mahayana path to reduce one's immediate suffering and increase one's ability to benefit sentient beings.

19. *Jamgön Kongtrul Lodrö Thayé* (1813-1899): One of the most prominent Buddhist masters in Tibet in the 19th century. He is credited as one of the founders of the Rime movement of

Tibetan Buddhism and compiled what is known as the *Five Great Treasuries*. He achieved great renown as a scholar and writer, and authored more than one hundred volumes of scriptures.

Section Two

20. *Precious Garland*: Written by Nagarjuna and belonging to his *Collection of Advice*. In the *Precious Garland*, Nagarjuna offers advice on how to conduct our lives and how to construct social policies that reflect Buddhist ideals.

21. *Entering into the Conduct of a Bodhisattva*: Also known as *Bodhicharyavatara*, Shantideva's classic guide to the Mahayana path composed of ten chapters dedicated to the development of bodhicitta (the mind of enlightenment) through the practice of the six perfections. Included among the so-called "thirteen great texts," which form the core of the curriculum in most monasteries.

Section Four

22. *Nagarjuna* (1st-2nd century A.D.): One of the principle founders of Mahayana Buddhism and the Indian philosopher who founded the Madhyamaka School after he systematized and deepened the teachings of the Perfection of wisdom sutras. Arguably the most influential Indian Buddhist thinker after Gautama Buddha, he provided the most comprehensive and methodological presentation of the Buddhist notion of emptiness.

23. *Atisha* (982-1054): Recognized as one of the greatest figures of classical Buddhism. His main disciple, Dromton, was the founder of the Kadam School. Atisha is also considered to be a key figure in the establishment of the Sarma schools of

Tibetan Buddhism

24. *Lamp of Enlightenment*: Written by Atisha and widely considered his magnum opus, also known as *Bodhipatha pradipa*. The text reconciles the doctrines of many various Buddhist schools and philosophies, and is notable for the introduction of the three levels of spiritual aspiration: lesser, middling, and superior, which in turn became the foundation for the Lamrim tradition.

Section Five

25. In the English translation, as a result of the difference in sentence structure between the two languages, the object is mentioned in the 4th line and the result in the 3rd line.

26. *Six Yogas of Naropa*: Also known as the Six Dharmas of Naropa (*naro cho druk*), sometimes also referred to simply as the Six Yogas (*cho druk*), are six sets of teachings and practices which originate from the Indian mahasiddha Naropa. They form the basis of the inner yoga practices of Mahamudra. They are: Inner heat (*candali, tummo*); Illusory body, (*mayakaya, gyu lu*); Clearlight/luminosity (*prabhasvara, osal*); Dream Yoga (*svapnadarsana, milam*); Transference of consciousness (*samkranti, phowa*); Yoga of the intermediate state, (*antarabhava, bardo*).

27. *Highest Continuum*: *Uttaratantra* or *Ratnagotravibhaga*. One of the Five Treatises of Maitreya, a commentary on the teachings of the third turning of the wheel of Dharma explaining buddha nature. It is included among the so-called "thirteen great texts."

28. *Wheel of Times*: also known as *Kalachakra*. See note 7.

29. *Yogacara*: Also known as *citta-matra* (mind-only), or

vijnanavada (consciousness school), is one of two major schools of Indian Mahayana Buddhism, the other being Madhyamaka. The founders of Yogacara, Asanga and his half brother Vasubandhu, believed Madhyamaka leaned too closely to nihilism by over emphasizing the emptiness of phenomena. Yogacara, meaning "one who practices yoga," is based on the third turning of the wheel by the Buddha and emphasizes the reality of the mind and Buddha-nature. It is influential in both Mahamudra and Dzogchen thought.

30. *Avadhut*: One of the mahasiddhas and the disciple of the the mahasiddha poet Kanhapa.

31. *Letter to a Friend*: Nagarjuna wrote his celebrated poem *Letter to a Friend* as a letter of advice to his friend King Gautamiputra Satakarni. This advice gives a concise and comprehensive introduction to the entire path and practice of Buddhism. It guides both householders and the ordained onto the path leading to liberation and enlightenment. The instructions are of special interest to those who wish to take up spiritual activity while continuing to live and work in society; they are meant to convey the whole meaning of the Dharma to the ordinary person in a language and style that are easy to understand.

32. *Shantideva*: (695–743) Indian Buddhist scholar from Nalanda University. An adherent of the Prasangika Madhyamaka philosophy and renowned as the author of *A Guide to the Bodhisattva's Way of Life*, a verse poem about the Mahayana path to enlightenment.

33. *Enlightenment of Vairocana*: An important Vajrayana text generally considered to be the root text of the Kriya class of Tantra and a comprehensive exposition of tantric practices in relationship to a set of deities, with Vairocana as the central deity.

34. *Phakmo Drupa*: (1110-1170) One of the three main disciples of Gampopa who established the Dagpo Kagyü school of Tibetan Buddhism, and a disciple of Sachen Kunga Nyingpo (1092-1158) one of the founders of the Sakya school of Tibetan Buddhism.

35. *Hevajra*: A Tantra of twenty chapters, thought to have originated in the eighth century. The *Hevajra Tantra* teaches the Union of Skillful Means and Wisdom. It is one of the Anuttarayoga Tantras, the highest of four classes of tantra in the Sarma or new schools of Tibetan Buddhism.

36. *Kandrel Pemachen*: This text is not identified.

37. *Heart Sutra*: The Heart Sutra is a teaching by the Bodhisattva Avalokitesvara, the Buddha of Compassion, to the monk Shariputra. Although very brief, The Heart Sutra contains key concepts of Buddhist Philosophy. These include the skandhas, the four noble truths, the cycle of interdependence, and the central concept of Mahayana Buddhism, emptiness.

38. *Diamond Pinnacle Tantra*: A supplementary text, surviving only in Tibetan translation and considered to be the main representative of the Yoga Tantra class of texts.

39. *Guhyasamaja tantra*: An important text of the Father Tantras of Vajrayana Buddhism.

40. *Ornament of Realization*: One of five Mahayana sutras which, according to Tibetan tradition, Maitreya revealed to Asanga. It summarizes all the topics in Prajnaparamita Sutras.

Section Six

41. *Bodhisattvabhumi*: Mahayana Buddhist text by Asanga laying down the stages (*bhumis*) of the path of the bodhisattva. It is the most comprehensive manual on the practice and training

of bodhisattvas.

42. *Five skandhas* or *five aggregates*: (*panca-skandha, phung po lnga*). The self is a collection of aggregates or psychophysical constituents. No single aggregate can be identified as the self; we simply have a notion of a self when all these aggregates come together. The five aggregates are the physical body (*rupa-skandha, gzugs kyi phung po*), feelings (*vedana-skandha, tshor ba'i phung po*), habitual dispositions (*samskara-skandha, 'du byed kyi phung po*), consciousness (*vijnana-skandha, rnam shes kyi phung po*), and perceptual experience (*samjna-skandha, 'du shes kyi phung po*).

Bibliography

The works listed appear in the order in which they are first mentioned in the book. In most cases, the English title is used in the body of the book. Where a commonly used abbreviation of the full Tibetan name may be more familiar to the reader than the full name, this has been included in the list rather than the full name. The abbreviated names have been spelled phonetically with the full name transliterated.

Questions of the Naga King Anavatapta, Madröpé Zhupai Do (Wylie: *ma dros pas zhus pa'i mdo*), *Anavataptanāgarājaparipṛcchāsūtra* (Skt.)

Candragomin. *Twenty Vows, Dompa Nyishupa* (Wylie: *sdom pa nyi shu pa*), *Saṃvaraviṃśaka* (Skt.)

Candrakīrti. *Entering the Middle Way, Uma Jukpa,* (Wylie: *dbu ma 'jug pa*), *Madhyamakāvatāra* (Skt.)

Nāgārjuna. *Precious Garland, Rinchen Trengwa* (Wylie: *rin chen phreng ba*), *Ratnāvali* (Skt.)

Śāntideva. *Entering the Conduct of a Bodhisattva, Chöjuk* (Wylie: *byang chub sems dpa'i spyod pa la 'jug pa*)—(abbreviated Tibetan name spelled phonetically, full name transliterated), *Bodhicaryāvatāra* (Skt.)

Atiśa Dīpaṃkaraśrījñāna. *Lamp of Enlightenment, Jangchup Lamgyi Drönma* (Wylie: *byang chub lam gyi sgron ma*), *Bodhipathapradīpa* (Skt.)

Enlightenment of Vairocana, Nampar Nangdzé Ngönpar Jangchupai

Gyü (Wylie: rnam par *snang mdzad mngon par byang chub pa'i rgyud*), *Mahāvairocanābhisambodhi* (Skt.)

Maitreya. *Highest Continuum, Gyü Lama* (Wylie: *rgyud bla ma*), *Uttaratantra* or *Ratnagotravibhāga* (Skt.)

Wheel of Time, Dükyi Khorlo (Wylie: *dus kyi 'khor lo*), *Kālachakra* (Skt.)

Nāgārjuna. *Letter to a Friend, Shetring* (Wylie: *bshes pa'i sprin yig*)—(abbreviated Tibetan name spelled phonetically, full name transliterated), *Suhṛllekha* (Skt.)

Kandrel Pemachen, (Wylie: *dka' grel padma can*)—text not identified

Heart Sutra, *Sherap Nyingpo*, (Wylie: *shes rab kyi pha rol tu phyin pa'i snying po*)—(abbreviated Tibetan name spelled phonetically, full name transliterated), *Prajñāpāramitā hṛdaya* (Skt.)

Diamond Pinnacle Tantra, Dorjé Tsemo Gyü (Wylie: *rdo rje rtse mo'i rgyud*) *Vajraśekhara tantra* (Skt.)

Sangwa Dupa, (Wylie: *gsang ba dus pa*), *Guhyasamāja tantra* (Skt.)

Maitreya. *Ornament of Realization, Ngöntok Gyen*, (Wylie: *shes rab kyi pha rol tu phyin pa'i man ngag gi bstan bcos mngon par rtogs pa'i rgyan zhes bya ba'i tshig le'ur byas pa*)—(abbreviated Tibetan name spelled phonetically, full name transliterated), *Abhisamayālaṅkāra* (Skt.)

Asaṅga. *Bodhisattva Levels, Naljor Chöpai Salé Jangchup Sempai Sa* (Wylie: *rnal 'byor spyod pa'i sa las byang chub sems dpa'i sa*) *Bodhisattvabhūmi* (Skt.)

Terms and Names

The following is a table of the phonetic spelling of Sanskrit names and terms used throughout the book matched with the terms transliterated according to the International Alphabet of Sanskrit Transliteration (IAST) system. They are listed in the order they first occur in the book.

As spelled in main body of book	With diacritical marks
Mahamudra	Mahāmudrā
Chandrakirti	Candrakīrti
paramita	parāmitā
nirmanakaya	nirmānakāya
sambhogakaya	saṃbhogakāya
dharmakaya	dharmakāya
svabhavikakaya	svabhāvikakāya
Hinayana	Hīnayāna
Mahayana	Mahāyāna
Vajrayana	Vajrayāna
upadesha	upadeśa
tathata	tathātā
rupa	rūpa
pratityasamutpada	pratītyasamutpāda
arya	ārya
paramita	pāramitā
Atisha	Atiśa
shamatha	śamatha
vipashyana	vipaśyanā
abhisheka	abhiṣeka
alayavijnana	ālayavijñāna

As spelled in main body of book	With diacritical marks
asamskrita	asaṃskṛta
alaya	ālaya
Avadhut	Avadhūti (abbreviated form of Avadhūtipāda)
amanasikara	amanasikāra
Manjushri	Mañjuśrī
Hevajra	Hevajra
mudra	mudrā
maha	mahā
karmamudra	karmamudrā
jnanamudra	jñānamudrā
Nagarjuna	Nāgārjuna

The following is a table of the phonetic spelling of Tibetan terms used throughout the book matched with the terms transliterated according to the Wylie transliteration system. Though often no precise English equivalent for a Tibetan term exists, an English translation has been provided for each term. These have been from Traleg Rinpoche's explanation of their meaning in the context of this book.

As spelled in main body of book	Wylie transliteration	English translation
jitawa	ji lta ba	the wisdom that apprehends the nature of things
jinyepa	ji snyed pa	the wisdom that perceives the extent of things
chö	chod	cutting through (lineage)
chö	chos	truth, scripture, secular law, social custom
depa	dad pa	faith
tsöndru	brtson 'grus	endeavor or vigor

As spelled in main body of book	Wylie transliteration	English translation
sherap	shes rab	intelligence or insight
döpai depa	'dod pa'i dad pa	admiration (form of faith)
dangway depa	dang ba'i dad pa	strong interest or longing
yichepai depa	yid ches pa'i dad pa	trusting faith
michepai depa	mi phyed pa'i dad pa	incontrovertible faith
gewai shenyen	dge ba'i bshes gnyen	spiritual friend
ka	bka'	oral discourses of the Buddha
tenchö	bstan bcos	Buddhist commentarial material
thöjung gi sherap	thos byung gi shes rab	insight arising from hearing
mengak	man ngag	oral instructions
samjung gi sherap	bsam byung gi shes rab	insight arising from contemplation
gomjung gi sherap	bsgoms byung gi shes rab	insight arising from practice of meditation
dewa chenpo zuk	bde ba chen po gzugs	body of great bliss
shi	gzhi	ground (of being)
kunzhi nampar shepa	kun gzh'i rnam par shes pa	storehouse consciousness or unconscious mind
dumajé	'dus ma byas	unconditioned phenomena
karpo chik thup	dkar po chig thub	panacea
yila mijepa	yid la mi byed pa	letting go
chakgya	phyag rgya	mudra
chenpo	chen po	great
sangyé	sangs rgyas	buddha, awakened

Glossary

Abhidharma: The series of discourses organized into texts by subject on Buddhist psychology and metaphysics. Buddhist teachings are often divided into 3 main sections: the sutras (teachings of the Buddha himself); the Vinaya (teachings on conduct, more especially guidance for the monastics); and the Abhidharma which are predominantly commentarial texts that analyze phenomena.

Abhisheka: In order to be able to practice a sadhana (tantric text and its associated ritual practicing such as visualization) one needs to receive a proper empowerment by an appropriately qualified teacher. According to Jamgon Kongtrul the Great, the Sanskrit word abhisheka derives from two sources. The first is abhikensa, meaning "sprinkling.. With every empowerment the teacher is purifying, or sprinkling a blessing of purification. The second word is *abkenta* which means putting something into a container. Jamgon Kongtrul explained that this referred to the process of being cleansed of defilements thus becoming a suitable vessel for the containment of wisdom.

Absolute Truth: (*dondam*) Transcends duality and sees things as they truly are, empty of inherent existence. For a fuller explanation see the *Two Truths*.

Alayavijnana: Is often translated as storehouse consciousness (Professor Guenther translated it as substratum of awareness) and is an important aspect of Yogacaran philosophical theory to explain the different levels of consciousness. Alayavijnana or storehouse consciousness is considered by the Yogacaran's to be ethically neutral and it is within this level of consciousness where mental imprints, such as memories, one's dispositional tendencies, and past traces and impressions are contained or stored. These imprints, traces and dispositions can be described as somewhat unconscious, potentially inactive or dormant (and can remain dormant for some time). With interactions with other levels of consciousness, such as the sense consciousnesses or Vijnana (our everyday responsiveness to our conscious experiences apprehended via the senses such as sight and hearing that in turn leave impressions and imprints in the Alayavijnana), when appropriate circumstances arise they can provoke the dormant traces and dispositions which compel us to act. From the Yogacaran's perspective this philosophical stance helps to explain what continues from one rebirth to the next. Buddhism does not believe in a permanent self, soul or atman, but equally supports the idea of the potential for purification, transformation, and enlightenment. Thus through meditation practices such as purification, and transformation, transcendental actions through ethical conduct and other disciplines within the Buddhist tradition, it is believed one can become conscious of the content within the Alayavijana. Such awareness helps to liberate oneself from such unconscious predetermined responsive constraints.

Awareness: (*jneya, shes bzhin*). The process of being alert and perspicacious. This type of awareness is deliberately generated in meditation practice as the principle means of accessing the innate wisdom consciousness.

Buddha: (*sangs rgyas*). Someone who has eliminated emotional and cognitive obscurations and achieved full enlightenment.

Bodhicitta: (*byang chub kyi sems*). Literally "enlightened heart," this is something we can only generate by thinking about the welfare of others in the cultivation of wisdom and compassion.

Bodhisattva: (*byang chub sems dpa'*). Literally an "awakening being" who has committed themselves to the path of compassion and the practice of the six paramitas while dedicating their actions to the welfare of all beings (See also transcendental perfections).

Compassion: (*karuna, snying rjes*). The wish that other beings may be free from suffering and the cause of suffering. It is materialized through the transcendental perfections of generosity, moral precepts, patience, and vigor and is the cause of leading an effective and fulfilling life.

Dharmakaya: see explanation under *Kaya*.

Emptiness: (*sunyata, stong pa nyid*). The understanding that persons, phenomena, and conceptual frameworks are devoid of any inherent existence. This description however should not lead one to a nihilistic view but rather a recognition of the lack of any truly existing independent nature of any or all phenomena. Phenomena do exist, however how they are apprehended and experienced is dependent on the receiver's predilections and in this respect are illusory. From a positive perspective due to emptiness, with the appropriate causes and conditions all things can come into existence. Further, due to the changeable and insubstantial nature of all things we live in a dynamic world (as opposed to a static one). From a personal perspective that means that we can change, improve, and transform.

Enlightenment: (*bodhi, byang chub*). Literally "the awakened state," it comes to completion with the development of compassion and the commitment to skillful means in order to liberate all sentient beings. The final fruition of complete liberation transcends all duality and conceptualization.

Geshé: A geshé is a Tibetan Buddhist academic degree for monks and nuns. The degree is emphasized primarily by the Gelug lineage. The geshé degree requires many years of intensive and rigorous academic study.

Ignorance: (*moha, gti mug*). An erroneous way of understanding, based on a lack of awareness where we go about our business in a mindless and inattentive fashion without being fully conscious of what we are feeling, thinking, and doing and thereby attributing an existence to beings and things that is solid, real, independent, and inherently existing.

Karma: (*las*). Literally "action," this is the unerring law of cause and effect, where positive actions bring happiness and negative actions bring suffering.

Kaya: There are four kayas: Kaya is often translated as body. *Dharmakaya, Nirmanakaya, Sambkogakaya,* and *Svabhavi kakaya*. Their meaning in brief: Dharmakaya can be described as an indeterminate, immaterial, and undifferentiated state of primal purity from which Nirmanakaya and Sambhogakaya arise. The purity remains untainted however to have access to it one needs to overcome or purify mental obscurations, conceptual confusions and the like. It is when the mind is purified that the Sambhogakaya aspect (continuous state of bliss) can manifest. It is a gateway of communication to others with minds purified sufficiently to see the enlightened manifestations. Nirmanakaya is the physical manifestation of a Buddha for the purpose of them relating to and communication with all beings for the purpose of benefiting others. The Nirmanakaya body is free of karmic residue. The three Kayas (or the three bodies of Buddha's being) Dharmakaya, Nirmanakaya, Sambkogakaya should not be seen as independent from one another. The fourth kaya, Svabhavikakaya is the interdependent unification of the three kaya.

Liberation: (*moksa, tharpa*). This is the final release from the cycle of death and rebirth and all the suffering and limitation of worldly existence.

Mahayana: (*dbu ma*): Literally means "great vehicle." The teachings of this phase of Buddhism arose several hundred years after the Buddha's paranirvana (passing) and emphasize emptiness (*shunyata*), compassion, and a universal buddha nature. It is often referred to as *the second turning of the wheel of dharma*. In the Mahayana tradition, the purpose of enlightenment is to liberate others, all sentient beings from suffering as well as oneself. Mahayana spread throughout Asia to China, Tibet, and Japan and became the established form of Buddhism in those countries.

Middle view: (*madhyam-drsti, dbu ma'i lta ba*). The understanding of Dependent Origination where we neither latch onto a metaphysical concept of the self nor deny the existence of such a concept. If we fail to hold the middle view, we might also fall into the extreme of upholding absolute reality at the expense of relative reality or vice versa.

Nirmanakaya: see explanation under *Kaya*.

Nirvana: (*samvrti-satya, kun rdzob bden pa*). Characterized as the cessation of suffering, nirvana is the goal of spiritual practice in Buddhism, signifying liberation from cyclic existence and the exhaustion of karma.

Relative truth: (*deva, lha*). The level of phenomenal appearances that are explained by Dependent Origination and synonymous with "how things appear." For a more detailed explanation see the *Two Truths*.

Sambkogakaya: see explanation under *Kaya*.

Samsara: (*anitya, mi rtag pa*). This is the idea that the transient nature of everything is the fundamental property of every conditioned thing. This fact is the basis of life because without it, existence would not be possible.

Shamatha: Shamatha meditation is also referred to as tranquility meditation and calm abiding. The main purpose of shamatha meditation is to relax and stabilize the mind by using a unitary focus such as the breath to allow the activity of the mind to settle. This is done for the primary purpose of preparing the mind to practice vipashyana or insight meditation. The practise of shamatha meditation is common to most schools of Buddhism.

shi: Ground of being, also translated as *gzhi, alaya*.

Svabhavikakaya: see explanation under *Kaya*.

Three Poisons: these are anger, attachment, and ignorance. For a more detailed explanation see *Samsara*.

Tranquility meditation: (shamatha, zhi gnas). A basic meditation practice, the aim of which is to tame and stabilize. For more explanation see *Shamatha*.

Two Accumulations: the two accumulations refers to the accumulation of both merit and wisdom. Merit refers predominantly to developing positive habits within one's intentions and actions. With continued effort the positive, ethical intentions and actions accumulate as inner riches. Wisdom refers to the development of insight into the human and sentient condition and the nature of reality. The accumulation of wisdom is achieved predominantly through Vipashyana or analytical meditational techniques. See also *Emptiness, Wisdom,* and *Wisdom mind*.

Two Truths: refers to the *ultimate* or *absolute* truth and *relative* or *conventional* truth. Ultimate or absolute truth refers to the untainted perception of ultimate reality or emptiness (the insubstantial and changeable nature of all things), by means of intuitive understanding, insight, and wisdom. Relative or conventional truth refers to the perception of the world as it exists including distorted ways of apprehending the world as static and inherently existing. Early Buddhist scholar Nagarjuna made the point that it is through relative truth that we come to develop an understanding of ultimate truth. Through this understanding one can develop the middle view avoiding the extremes of eternalism and nihilism. Also the two-truths have the same nature, that of emptiness.

Vinaya: One of the three sections of the Buddhist Canon, along with Sutra and Abhidharma, it contains the rules of the Buddhist order and the vows of the Buddhist monastics.

Vipashyana: Vipashyana meditation also known as analytical meditation uses a range of techniques to build insight into how the mind works and the nature of reality. See also *Emptiness*.

Wisdom: (*prajna, shes rab*). Wisdom is cultivated through the development of concentration, contemplation, and insight or analytical meditation also known as Vipashyana, and is the cause of direct insight into the reality of things as they are, free of extrapolation.

Wisdom mind: (*jnana, ye she*). An innate capacity of the mind, which gives rise to genuine insight when the obscurations of deluded consciousness are eradicated.

Index

Abhidharma, 21, 22,
abhishekas, 36
absolute, 11, 27, 34, 49–54, 57–58, 62
– absolute truth, 28–29, 96
accomplishment, 1, 5, 6, 19, 39, 97, 99
accumulation, 30, 31, 92, 99
action, xvii, 2, 7, 8–11, 39, 42,–43, 93, 97
adventitious defilements, 34–35, 38–39
agitation, 34, 69–70, 84, 86–87
alaya, 32, 57
Alayavjnana, 45–47, 57
all-encompassing, 74, 80
aspiration, xxii, 5, 14–15, 19, 21, 72, 95–96, 99
awareness, 44, 46, 50, 58, 60, 66, 69, 71, 79, 86–87

Bodhisattva, 7, 15, 74, 95, 97
Buddha, 7–8, 11–12, 14, 21, 23–24, 31–32, 48, 89, 95, 97
– buddhahood, 3, 5, 32, 49, 56–57, 92, 94, 97–99
– buddha nature 40, 89
– buddha realms, 94, 95

causes and conditions, 28–29, 55, 66
Chandrakirti, 22, 48
co-emergent wisdom, 53–54, 78
compassion, 5–7, 10–11, 14, 30–32, 88–92, 95, 99

conceptuality, 53, 82, 84–85, 98
– concept, 27–28, 43, 46, 48, 51–52, 87–88, 90
– conceptual, 21, 32, 41, 50, 54–55, 67–68, 71, 73–76, 82–83, 86– 88, 90, 96
conditioned, 50–52, 54–56, 63, 71–72, 86, 97
confidence, 2, 4, 16–17, 23–24, 39, 41, 55, 76–77
conscious, 28, 56, 68, 83–84
– consciousness, 34–36, 40–41, 43–50, 55–57, 59, 72
contemplate, 20, 23
– contemplating, 2, 20, 22–23, 30
– contemplation, 22–23, 25, 30, 37
cultivate, 29, 33, 41, 83, 85–86, 91–92

dakinis, 6
definitive, 18
deities, 1, 6, 36–37, 65–67, 81
deluded, xix, 15, 34–35, 41, 46, 48
delusion, 32, 35, 47, 48
dependent arising, 28
dependent origination, 28
Dharma, xx, 20, 46
dharmakaya, 2, 11, 32–33, 39, 48, 77–78
dharmata, xxii, 5, 85, 88
distraction, 60, 63, 86
dullness, 4, 67–69

Dzogchen, xxiii, xxv, 4, 6, 76–78
empirical, 39, 44, 46, 49, 52, 54–55, 58, 60, 72
- empirical consciousness, 35, 40, 49, 71
- empirical mind, 34
empowerment, 36, 38
emptiness, 1, 28–29, 34–35, 38, 46, 51–54, 58, 73, 79–80, 82–84, 87–91
enlightened, 5, 12, 14, 24, 31–32, 40, 46, 50–51, 57, 61, 88–89, 94–97
enlightenment, 11, 14, 29–31, 40, 48, 56–57, 59, 74–75, 79, 94–95, 99
essence, xviii, 2–5, 7, 11, 18, 29, 33, 44, 46, 54, 62, 65, 70, 72–73, 76–78, 87, 90
  enduring essence, 27–30, 74
eternalism, 2, 26–28, 30, 32, 51, 76
ethical, 7, 8, 21
exist, 9, 12, 27–29, 35, 38, 43–44, 48–49, 52–54, 58–59, 72, 78, 90
extreme, 27–28, 30, 34, 52, 56, 69, 76
- extremes, 2–4, 26–27, 30–32, 49, 51, 53, 56, 76–77

faith, xxii, 1, 15, 16, 17, 22
five obstacles, 69
fixation, 3–4, 44, 47, 72–73, 82, 85
four Kayas, 1, 7, 11, 12
fruition, xx, 2, 13, 26, 31–33, 42, 58–59, 94, 97

great bliss, 4, 24, 53–54, 82
ground, 2, 4, 26, 32–33, 39–41, 43, 56–59
- ground Mahamudra, 58–59
- ground of being, 26–27, 30, 32

ignorance, 2–3, 15, 18, 22, 44, 46–47, 56–57, 89, 97
immaculate mind, 35
insight, 13–14, 16–18, 20, 22–25, 29, 36, 39, 42–43, 48, 58, 71, 74–75, 82, 89–92, 97–98
- insight meditation, 41, 70, 72
intention, 7–10, 18, 79, 89–90
interdependent, 9
intrinsically pure, 34

Kagyü, xviii–xix, xxi–xxv, 6, 8, 35, 37–38, 64
- Kagyupa, 77, 87
kaya, 12
  four kayas, 1, 7, 11, 12
  three kayas, 12

lamp, 31, 51, 90–91
letting go, 79
liberation, 10, 18, 47, 59–60, 65, 91
- self-liberation, 65
logic, 22, 54, 75
luminosity, 4, 34–35, 46, 50–51,

74, 82–84, 90–91, 98

madhyamaka, 52, 76–77, 89
Maha Ati, 76, 78
Mahayana, xx, 8–10, 18, 27, 38, 40, 50, 57, 69–70, 74–78, 89–92, 98–99
meditate, 61
   – meditation, xviii–xix, 2–3, 7, 10, 18, 20–21, 23–25, 30–31, 33, 36–37, 39, 41–42, 55–56, 59, 60–71, 74–76, 79, 82–86, 88–89, 93, 98–99
   – meditator, 41, 51–52, 58, 60–75, 79, 82–89, 91–98
mentation, 79, 80
metaphor, 9, 12
middle view, 27, 52, 53
   – middle way, 3–4, 10, 49, 76–77
mirror-like wisdom, 39, 97
moral, 7–8, 21, 27, 29–30, 32, 53

Nagarjuna, xix–xx, 28, 52, 69, 89
natural, xviii–xix, 2, 4, 20, 23–25, 42, 62–66, 68, 70, 72, 74, 80, 83–84, 86–89
nature of the mind, 11, 24, 33–35, 37–44, 46, 48–60, 62, 64, 66, 70–72, 74–75, 77, 81, 87–88
nihilism, 28, 30, 76
nirmanakaya, 11, 12, 96
nirvana, xix, 3, 11, 24, 31–32, 47, 49, 51, 77, 80, 91, 98
non-conceptuality, 98, 99

non-meditation, xvii, 98, 99
Nyingma, xxii, xxiv–xxv, 6,

obstacles, 1, 15, 19, 34, 41, 69–70, 83–84, 86
   – two obstacles, 69
   – two primary obstacles, 69
   – five obstacles, 69
ordinary mind, 5, 85–87

paramita, 10
path, xviii, xxii, 2, 5, 8,–9, 12–15, 17–18, 20, 25–26, 32–34, 37, 41, 51, 56, 58–59, 78, 85, 90, 92–95, 97–99
   path Mahamudra, 59
practitioner, 6, 7, 9, 11, 13–18, 23, 25–27, 29–32, 37, 39, 55, 58–60, 62–63, 66, 76–79, 81, 88, 91
Prajnaparamita, 77
phenomena, 2, 29, 42–44, 54–55, 87
purification, 2, 33–35, 38, 56, 96–97

reality, xviii, 14, 17, 21, 24–30, 32, 43, 46, 55–56, 58, 73–84, 89–92, 98
realize, xix, 2–5, 29, 33–34, 37, 43, 47, 49, 53–55, 57, 59, 65–67, 71–72, 74–78, 85, 88
relative, 11, 18, 21, 48–50, 52, 57–58
   – relative truth, 14, 27–29, 32, 96

- relative aspect, 50–52, 57, 59–60, 62
riches, 1, 8, 15–16
right view, 40–4, 89
ripening, 5, 94, 95, 97
Rupa, 24

Sambhogakaya, 11–12
samsara, xix, 3, 5, 10–11, 29, 32, 40, 45–47, 49, 51, 56, 77, 80, 88, 91, 98
 - samsaric, 3, 14, 32, 36, 44, 46–47, 51, 56–59, 81, 89, 91
Saraha, xviii–xxi
self-cognition, 50
sentient being, 14, 40, 56, 57
 - sentient beings, 5, 40, 47–50, 56, 58, 88–89, 95–96
shamatha, 4, 36, 41, 62–63, 67–68, 70–71, 76
shi, 32
six paramitas, 29, 31
 - six transcendental actions, 29, 31
skill-in-means, 10–11
stabilized mind, 60
storehouse-consciousness, 45–47, 57
sutra, xviii, 7, 18, 50, 74, 78, 80, 87, 91
 - sutric, 38, 40, 52, 75–76, 87–88, 97–99
svabhavikakaya, 11, 12

tantra, xviii–xix, 90–91

 - tantric, xviii–xix, xxii–xxiii, 36–38, 40, 42, 46–48, 65–67, 76, 77–78, 80–81, 91, 93, 97
 - tantrism, 38, 93
three-term relationship, 10, 11
three times, 1, 64, 65
transcendental action, 10, 31
true nature, 72, 77
 - true face, 72
two accumulations, 2, 26, 30–32
two benefits, 2, 26, 31
two-fold purity, 39
two truths, 2, 26, 27

ultimate reality, xviii, 14, 21, 24–27, 29, 32, 74–84, 88–92, 98
 - ultimate truth, 14, 21, 27–29, 32, 97
unconditioned, 3, 49–55, 66, 71

vajra, 2, 33, 65
view, xxiv, 2-3, 27–29, 32, 34–35, 39–44, 51–55, 57–58, 63, 72, 82, 85, 88, 93, 96–98
vigilant, 15, 30
vigor, 16, 17
vinaya, xxiii, 21–22, 77
vipashyana, 70–71, 7–76
voidness, 79

wisdom, 10–11, 14, 20, 22, 24–26, 30–32, 36, 39, 48, 50, 53–54, 57, 77–78, 88, 90–92, 96–97

Yogacara, 75